TEENS & Gay Issues

HAL MARCOVITZ

THE GALLUP YOUTH SURVEY:
MAJOR ISSUES AND TRENDS

Teens and Alcohol

Teens and Career Choices

Teens and Cheating

Teens and Family Issues

Teens, Health, and Obesity

Teens and Homosexuality

Teens and the Media

Teens and Race

Teens and Relationships

Teens, Religion, and Values

Teens and Sex

Teens and Suicide

Teens and the Supernatural/Paranormal

Teens and Volunteerism

TEENS &
Gay Issues

HAL MARCOVITZ

Produced by OTTN Publishing, Stockton, New Jersey

Mason Crest Publishers
370 Reed Road
Broomall, PA 19008
www.masoncrest.com

3 5 7 9 8 6 4 2

Library of Congress Cataloging-in-Publication Data

Marcovitz, Hal.
   Teens and gay issues / Hal Marcovitz.
      p. cm. — (The Gallup Youth Survey, major issues and trends)
   Includes bibliographical references and index.
   ISBN 1-59084-873-X
   1. Gay youth—United States—Juvenile literature. 2. Gay rights—United
States—Juvenile literature. 3. Homosexuality—Juvenile literature. I. Title. II.
Series.
   HQ76.26.M37 2005
   305.235—dc22
                              2004013755

Contents

Introduction

By George Gallup

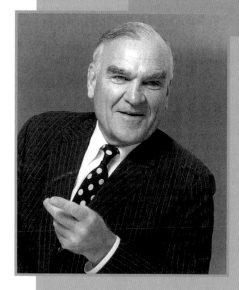

As the United States moves into the new century, there is a vital need for insight into what it means to be a young person in America. Today's teenagers—the so-called "Y Generation"—will be the leaders and shapers of the 21st century. The future direction of the United States is being determined now in their hearts and minds and actions. Yet how much do we as a society know about this important segment of the U.S. populace who have the potential to lift our nation to new levels of achievement and social health?

The nation's teen population will top 30 million by the year 2006, the highest number since 1975. Most of these teens will grow up to be responsible citizens and leaders. But some youths face very long odds against reaching adulthood physically safe, behaviorally sound, and economically self-supporting. The challenges presented to society by the less fortunate youth are enormous. To help meet these challenges it is essential to have an accurate picture of the present status of teenagers.

The Gallup Youth Survey—the oldest continuing survey of teenagers—exists to help society meet its responsibility to youth, as well as to inform and guide our leaders by probing the social and economic attitudes and behaviors of young people. With theories abounding about the views, lifestyles, and values of adolescents, the Gallup Youth Survey, through regular scientific measurements of teens themselves, serves as a sort of reality check.

We need to hear more clearly the voices of young people, and to help them better articulate their fears and their hopes. Our youth have much to share with their elders—is the older generation really listening? Is it carefully monitoring the hopes and fears of teenagers today? Failure to do so could result in severe social consequences.

Surveys reveal that the image of teens in the United States today is a negative one. Teens are frequently maligned, misunderstood, or simply ignored by their elders. Yet two decades of the Gallup Youth Survey have provided ample evidence of the very special qualities of the nation's youngsters. In fact, if our society is less racist, less sexist, less polluted, and more peace loving, we can in considerable measure thank our young people, who have been on the leading edge on these issues.

And the younger generation is not geared to greed: survey after survey has shown that teens have a keen interest in helping those people, especially in their own communities, who are less fortunate than themselves

Young people tell the Gallup Youth Survey that they are enthusiastic about helping others, and are willing to work for world peace and a healthy world. They feel positive about their schools and even more positive about their teachers. A large majority of American teenagers report that they are happy and excited about the future, feel very close to their families, are likely to marry, want to have children, are satisfied with their personal lives, and desire to reach the top of their chosen careers.

But young adults face many threats, so parents, guardians, and concerned adults must commit themselves to do everything possible to help tomorrow's parents, citizens, and leaders avoid or overcome risky behaviors so that they can move into the future with greater hope and understanding.

The Gallup Organization and the Gallup Youth Survey are enthusiastic about this partnership with Mason Crest Publishers. Through carefully and clearly written books on a variety of vital topics dealing with teens, Gallup Youth Survey statistics are presented in a way that gives new depth and meaning to the data. The focus of these books is a practical one—to provide readers with the statistics and solid information that they need to understand and to deal with each important topic.

* * *

This book documents the changes that have come about in recent years in teen (and adult) attitudes on gay issues. Clearly there is far less of a stigma today in being gay than there was in the past. But sharp differences in attitudes remain on these issues. Two-thirds of teenagers agree with the statement that homosexuality should be considered an acceptable lifestyle, but one-third disagree or are undecided. In addition, 64 percent of teens disapprove of marriage between homosexuals, and opinions are evenly divided on the right of gay people to adopt children.

Teens and Gay Issues takes a comprehensive look at the issues faced by gay teenagers, addressing the "nature versus nurture" argument as well as problems faced by gays, such as higher levels of depression, suicide, and drug and alcohol use and a greater risk of being infected with the virus that causes AIDS.

Extrapolation of survey trends suggests that teen views of gay issues today will likely lead to a climate of increased respect for gays in society during the years ahead.

Chapter One

Chastity Bono is hugged by her mother, pop star Cher. As a teenager Chastity was afraid to tell her parents she was a lesbian. When her mother found out she did not react well at first, but over time Cher came to accept and support her daughter's lifestyle.

When Gay Teens Come Out

By the time she was 17 years old, Chastity Bono had told nearly all the people she knew that she is gay. Friends, classmates, a trusted aunt—everyone seemed to know that Chastity was a *lesbian*. However, there were two people whom Chastity had not told: her mother and father.

Chastity's mother is Cher, a singer and Academy Award–winning actress. Chastity's father, Sonny Bono, was a singer and songwriter who later became a U.S. congressman. During the 1960s and 1970s Sonny and Cher had been responsible for such hit songs as "I Got You Babe" and "The Beat Goes On," and had starred together on a popular television variety show. Chastity hoped one day to have a career in entertainment herself. As a young girl she often made appearances on her parents' television show, and by the time she was a teenager Chastity was writing songs and playing drums in a rock band.

When she was nearly 17, Chastity was finding it difficult to keep her homosexuality a secret from her parents. Chastity and a lesbian classmate named Julie were spending a lot of time together, and one night, Chastity's mother walked in on them kissing on the living room sofa. Startled and unsure of what she had just seen, Cher hurried out of the room and never asked her daughter about the incident. Chastity, however, could tell that her mother was suspicious and had suddenly grown cold toward her. A few weeks later, Cher refused to show up at her daughter's 17th birthday party because she knew Julie would be there. In her book *Family Outing*, Chastity wrote, "It wasn't until years later that my mom finally admitted to me her real reason for not coming to my birthday party: she was devastated after walking in on me and Julie."

Chastity found it far easier to talk to her father. By then, Sonny and Cher were divorced. One evening, Sonny took his daughter out for dinner. Sonny told Chastity he could tell she was troubled and assured her she could confide in him. "After hemming and hawing," she wrote, "I finally got up my courage and blurted, 'I'm gay.'" Sonny accepted the news and told his daughter she had his complete support.

Cher was not so willing to accept the truth about her daughter. When, finally, Chastity decided to confide in her mother, Cher grew angry and ordered her daughter to move out of their home. It would take a long time for Cher and Chastity to reconcile, but in the end Cher accepted her daughter's lifestyle.

"Telling our parents is the single most important and often most frightening part of coming out," Chastity wrote. "Most of us grow up wanting to please our parents. We want our parents to love us, and we fear disappointing them. No matter what kind of family we come from—whether it's a traditional nuclear family with a mother and father as heads of the household, or we have divorced parents, or we live in a tightly knit extended family—as soon as we realize we are gay we are presented with a conflict: we want to tell our family so that they know 'who we really are,' but we are also afraid to tell them for fear of rejection."

Chastity Bono is not unlike thousands of young people who discover they are gay and must decide whether to tell their friends and family members the truth. Years ago, most gay people refused to "come out" for fear of being ostracized in the community and at their places of employment, so they led secret lives. But times have changed in the United States. Today, men and women march in gay pride parades. Gay people publish their own newspapers and magazines. Openly gay citizens hold public office, serving on city councils, state legislatures, and in the U.S. Congress. Gay activists pressure lawmakers to adopt measures defining their rights as citizens. Popular television programs like *Will & Grace* feature gay characters. Most Americans say they respect gay people's rights and there is much less stigma attached to being gay than there was in the past.

This does not mean openly gay people do not face prejudice. Stories of harassment and abuse are often featured in the media. And gay people continue to struggle to win rights guaranteed to other Americans.

The Gallup Organization, a national polling firm, has often studied how teens view issues affecting gays through the Gallup Youth Survey, a longtime project by the firm to assess the ideas of young people in the United States. Over the years, the Gallup Youth Survey has found that teens' attitudes have changed toward gays, reflecting a trend by young people to be more accepting of the homosexual lifestyle. In 1979, for example, the

Gallup Youth Survey wanted to know whether young people believed gays should hold certain jobs. A total of 500 teens between the ages of 13 and 18 were asked whether gays should work as salespersons, soldiers, college professors, high school teachers, elementary school teachers, clergymen, and physicians. In an average of the seven professions tested, 54% of the respondents opposed gays holding jobs in those professions. An 18-year-old New Mexico boy gave a typical response. "They just give me the creeps," he told the Gallup researchers. "I guess it's all right for them to be in sales, but keep them out of anything that involves teaching — or preaching, for that matter. Those kinds of jobs give them too much of an opportunity to try to teach kids their way of life."

More than two decades later, attitudes had definitely changed. In 1998, a Gallup Youth Survey of 500 teens showed that 64 percent of the respondents agreed with the statement: "Homosexuality should be considered an acceptable lifestyle." And in 2000 and 2001, a Gallup Youth Survey found that 79 percent of U.S. teens said they "feel comfortable being with people whose ideas, beliefs, and values are different from their own."

This book will address many of the issues faced by gay teenagers as well as other young people. In addition to exploring the question of when and how gay teens come out, this book will discuss the issue of whether homosexuality is an inherited trait or whether young people turn to a gay lifestyle because of their environments. The ways in which gays are accepted in school and elsewhere in the community will be discussed, and the views of *bisexual* teens will be explored. Finally, this book will help young gays look into the future to see if they can expect to find a tolerant society awaiting them when they emerge from their teen years.

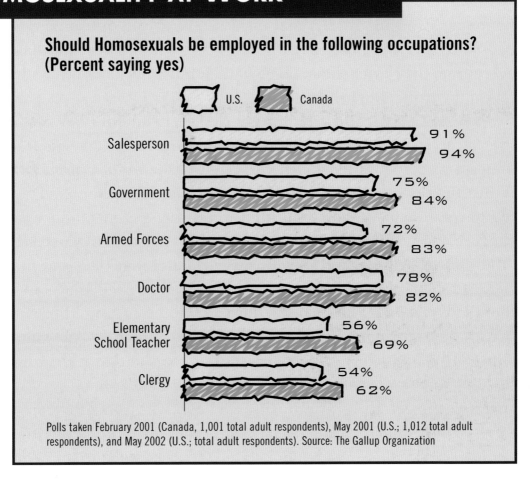

Should Homosexuals be employed in the following occupations? (Percent saying yes)

U.S.   Canada

Occupation	U.S.	Canada
Salesperson	91%	94%
Government	75%	84%
Armed Forces	72%	83%
Doctor	78%	82%
Elementary School Teacher	56%	69%
Clergy	54%	62%

Polls taken February 2001 (Canada, 1,001 total adult respondents), May 2001 (U.S.; 1,012 total adult respondents), and May 2002 (U.S.; total adult respondents). Source: The Gallup Organization

Letting the Secret Out

The term "coming out" is actually short for "coming out of the closet." A closet is a dark place where people often keep things they don't want others to see. There may be nothing wrong with what people hide in their closets; they simply prefer their friends not know what is in there. A gay person looks at his or her life as a closet. Before they come out, they live their lives in darkness, hiding a secret they prefer to keep from the people they know. Most gay people describe coming out as a liberating experience — exposing the truth to the light of day, no longer living in darkness, no longer guarding secrets that need not be secret. Yet some gay people believe the closet is with them their entire lives, and that every time they meet someone new, they must decide whether to reveal the truth about themselves.

Vanessa Duran came out at the age of 17. In an interview with the *Advocate*, a national news magazine devoted to gay issues, Vanessa said she fretted for months that her parents, particularly her fundamentalist Christian mother, would be horrified by the news. Finally, Vanessa decided to tell her parents, and was shocked to find a much different reaction than she had expected. "I told them I'm gay, and they busted up laughing," she told the *Advocate*. "We've come to a quiet understanding: they know, and there's no reason for me to bring it up again . . . My mom is growing to the understanding that I didn't leave church to become a sinner. I still have my beliefs and morals, so she doesn't rub in my face some quote she learned in church that evening."

Adolescence can be a confusing and awkward time for many teens as they undergo changes in their bodies, learn about dating, and experience their first relationships with the opposite sex. Gay teenagers not only face the pressures of adjusting to adolescence that all teens face, they must also come to terms with their sexuality. Still, gay teenagers feel the need to be honest about their sexuality to themselves and others. According to a report issued in 2001 by the civil rights group Human Rights Watch, "youth are 'coming out' — identifying themselves as gay, lesbian, bisexual or *transgender* — at younger ages."

The organization said that according to studies, girls have reported recognizing that they are lesbians at ages as young as 10 and have their first same-sex experience at the age of 15. Meanwhile, boys report finding themselves attracted to other boys at ages as young as nine and have said that their first same-sex experiences occurred at ages as young as 13. "Both girls and boys begin to identify themselves as lesbian or gay at age 16," the organization said.

Other groups have drawn similar conclusions. OutProud, a California-based gay youth support group, conducted Internet-based surveys in 1997 and 2000. Individuals between the ages of 10 and 25 responded to the surveys, although most respondents were identified as high school and college students. Here is what OutProud had to say about the results of its 2000 survey: "The typical individual was 12.4 years old when they realized that they were *queer*. However, it took them, on average, until they were 15.6 years old to accept this fact. And they didn't tell anyone until they

Young people take part in a Lesbian and Gay Pride Parade. Many organizations have been formed to help teens deal with the emotional trauma of coming out, or to fight discrimination against homosexuals.

were 16.1 years old, on average." What is so interesting is that a survey OutProud conducted just three years earlier found that the average age of gay youths who decided to come out was 16.3 years. Therefore, in the space of just three years, the average age of coming out had decreased by a few months, indicating that young gays have become more willing to come out to their parents and friends.

Old Prejudices

Those statistics indicate that young gay people do feel a sense of empowerment by coming out. And it is true that many gay teens find families and friends who are warm and understanding

AMERICA'S YOUNG GAY POPULATION

How many of America's 72 million young people are gay? It is not an easy question to answer. Over the years, surveys asking young people about their sexual preferences have produced a wide range of results. Most gay rights organizations believe that 10 percent of the male population of America is gay—an estimate first developed in 1947 by sex researcher Dr. Alfred Kinsey. Later, Kinsey concluded that 5 percent of the female population of America is gay. Since then, other researchers have said the number of gay Americans is probably lower.

In 1992, a survey of nearly 35,000 junior and senior high school students in Minnesota found that 1.1 percent of the students identified themselves as bisexual or homosexual. Later, a 1999 survey in Massachusetts produced somewhat higher numbers. In that study, 5.5 percent of young people identified themselves as gay or bisexual. And a 1995 study conducted in Vermont on risky sexual activity by young people found that 8.7 percent of boys in the 8th through 12th grades reported having had sex with other boys.

when they do come out. Chastity Bono and Vanessa Duran came out to parents and friends who were ultimately, if not immediately, supportive. Still, many teens find the opposite to be true. Even in a society that recognizes gay rights, old **prejudices** remain. Not all teens are as lucky as Chastity and Vanessa. In 1998, *Rolling Stone* interviewed a number of gay teenagers; many recounted stories of closed minds, hostile attitudes, and cold receptions.

Fifteen-year-old Tara Conroy told *Rolling Stone* that about a month after she came out, administrators at the Catholic school Tara attended called her parents and told them they were not comfortable with having a lesbian on campus. "I was so glad that I was out then, because if I hadn't been they would have outed me

In 2001, the National Longitudinal Study of Adolescent Health conducted by researchers at the University of North Carolina surveyed some 12,000 young people in the 7th through 12th grades and reported that just 1 percent expressed an interest in same-sex relationships.

The U.S. Census Bureau—the government agency in charge of developing statistics on the characteristics of the American population—does not conduct a comprehensive count of gay people. In 2000, however, the agency made an attempt to count the number of households headed by same-sex couples. That year, the Census Bureau found that of the 105,480,101 total households in the United States, 594,391 are headed by same-sex partners. Those numbers would indicate that about one-half of 1 percent of American households are headed by same-sex couples. That number included 301,026 households headed by male partners and 293,365 headed by female partners. Of course, those numbers exclude people under 18 and gay people who do not share their households with partners.

to my parents," Tara told *Rolling Stone*. "They would have literally said to them, 'Your daughter's a lesbian, and she's not welcome here.'" Another teen interviewed by *Rolling Stone*, 16-year-old Dylan Parker, said that after he came out, nobody at his high school—not even the girls—would talk to him. "That actually surprised me," Dylan said of the girls at his school. "Of all people, why should it bother them?" And high school junior Wendy Craig told *Rolling Stone* that after she came out to her parents, they kicked her out of the house. "For awhile, they'd been dropping hints about it," Wendy told the magazine. "I thought it was my parents saying, 'Come on and tell us, it's OK.' But as soon as I told them it was true, they were disgusted."

Cincinnati teenager Marie Hedrick told the *Advocate* about what she experienced when she came out at the age of 12. "Everyone seemed to know I was gay before I did," she said. "A lot of it was verbal. Kids would make accusations a lot or stop looking at me.

Basically there was an attitude of 'I know you want me' by the girls. There weren't really any teachers I could talk to, but I wasn't really good at reaching out for it either. If you are being harassed constantly, you don't really think of going to the teacher and saying, 'I'm being harassed constantly.'" Finally, Marie did speak with a guidance counselor at her school. "She told me that it was just a phase and that if I wore nicer clothes, other kids would like me more. I sort of looked at her. She said, 'I've studied these things.' And that was the end of the conversation."

And high school freshman Ryan Fischer said he faced hostility, but he also learned who his true friends were. "Coming out was hard and scary," Ryan wrote in an essay for *Upfront*, a publication of the *New York Times*. "We have **homophobic** people in our school, and being gay is not right or normal to them. Growing up, I was always asked if I was gay, and I always denied it. Still, people would physically and verbally abuse me, because they assumed I was gay. Eventually, my self-esteem fell so low that I didn't even want to live. I tried to kill myself a number of times, and was put on an antidepressant medication."

Finally, Ryan said, he came out to his parents and friends, and found them supportive. "One day I was walking out of school with a friend, and someone confronted her and called me a name," he wrote. "My friend got in his face and told him that I was one of her best friends, and if he ever tried messing with me, he would have to go through her first. It has shocked me that I've made new friends since I came out. Some students have asked to meet me because I'm gay and I seem nice."

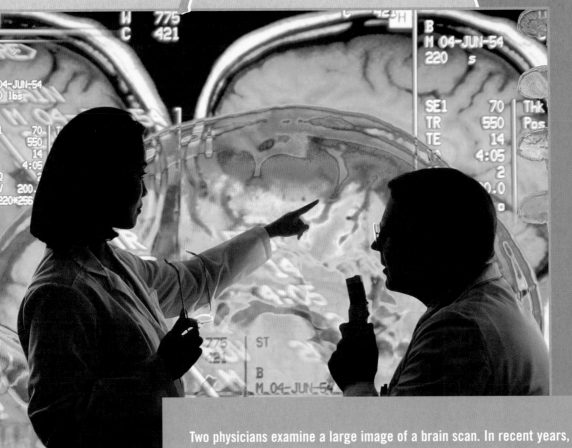

Chapter Two

Two physicians examine a large image of a brain scan. In recent years, research has indicated that there may be genetic or biological causes for homosexuality.

Nature or Nurture?

Growing up in Great Britain, Simon LaVay realized by the age of 12 that he was gay. Upon analysis of Simon's background, a psychologist may have agreed with this realization. That is because at the time homosexuality was believed to be a disease caused by external factors. Simon was bookish as a young boy and hated rough-and-tumble sports. He maintained a strong attachment to his mother, but found his father distant and hostile. However, although Simon ultimately concluded in his own mind that he was gay, he was not ready to believe that his environment and upbringing were wholly responsible for making him into a homosexual. Instead, LaVay suspected other causes.

Simon LaVay went on to become a research scientist, and by the early 1990s he was working at the California-based Salk Institute where he headed research projects that studied the human brain. In 1991, LaVay announced the results of a study that stunned gay people everywhere. After analyzing the brains of 41 *cadavers*, LaVay and his assistants concluded that a tiny section of the brain known as the hypothalamus was, in most cases, less than half the size in gay men than in *heterosexual* men. This discovery meant that there could be biological reasons for homosexuality: people were born with a physical trait that made them gay and, therefore, being gay was a result of "nature" and not a psychological reaction to one's environment. "It would reduce being gay to something like being left-handed, which is in fact all that it is," San Francisco gay activist Randy Shilts told *Newsweek* shortly after LaVay's findings were announced.

Since then many other researchers have looked for biological causes to homosexuality. Some scientists believe they have uncovered evidence suggesting the existence of a *gene* related to homosexuality that is passed down from generation to generation. Many gay activists welcomed the scientific developments, arguing that they showed a gay person had no more choice in his or her sexual preference than a black person had a choice in the color of his or her skin and, therefore, the nation's civil rights laws should apply to everyone, regardless of race, gender, or sexual preference. Other gay people worried that if a "gay gene" is ever isolated, then genetic engineers would attempt to alter the *DNA* content of a father's sperm or a mother's egg, eliminating the gay gene and ensuring that a son or daughter would grow up heterosexual. Jan Platner, head of an organization known as Gay and Lesbian Advocates and Defenders, had this to say to the Associated Press: "Some people look at being gay as a defect that should be changed but those who are gay don't see it that way."

Most adolescents who discover they are gay undoubtedly will soon ask themselves these questions: *why am I gay? Why am I different from my parents and my friends?* Even with the recent scientific research into the possible causes of homosexuality, those questions remain largely unanswered. Experts agree that even if a gay gene is isolated or Simon LaVay's work is confirmed through additional tests, there is still no single thread that can link all gay people to a common reason. They say the decision to lead a gay lifestyle could be based on any number of reasons, including genetic traits that are inherited from relatives as well as other biological factors, the environment in which the person grows up, and each person's psychological makeup. Dr. Dean H. Hamer, the Maryland scientist whose work linked homosexuality to DNA, warned that people should not

Such respected researchers in the field of human sexuality as William Masters and Virginia Johnson, authors of *Homosexuality in Perspective* (1979) among other works, believed that homosexuality is the product of experience, not genetics. Today, most experts believe that both components may factor into determining a person's sexuality.

misinterpret his findings to eliminate all other causes. "Genes are part of the story . . . but it's not all of the story," Hamer told *Time*.

A majority of teens appear to believe that a young person's environment has a lot to do with the decision to choose homosexuality. A Gallup Youth Survey in 2003 polled 1,200 teens between the ages of 13 and 17, asking them, "In your view, is homosexuality due to outside factors such as upbringing and environment, or is homosexuality something a person is born with?" Sixty-one percent of the respondents said they felt that environment is the key to homosexuality, while 36 percent thought sexual orientation is an inherited trait.

Teens who are regular churchgoers and are, perhaps, influenced by conservative religious leaders are more likely to believe the "nurture" theory and the notion that environment causes homosexuality. According to the Gallup Youth Survey, 71 percent of teens who attended church within the past seven days said they believe home life, upbringing, and similar factors cause homosexuality, while 27 percent of those teens favored the "nature" theory, meaning they believe people are born with a trait that makes them gay. As for teens who do not regularly attend church, a smaller majority, 54 percent, sided with the nurture theory, while a larger minority, 43 percent, agreed with the nature theory.

Politically conservative teens also favored the nurture theory, with 72 percent of young people who identified themselves as future Republicans saying they believe environment is the most significant cause of homosexuality, while 56 percent of future Democrats said they agreed with the nurture argument.

Seeking the Cure

When *Rolling Stone* interviewed gay teenagers in 1998, one high school senior named Sidney told the magazine that when he was between the ages of seven and 11, he had repeatedly been sexually assaulted by an older brother. Sidney told the magazine that he reported the assaults to his mother, who refused to believe him. "I'll never forgive her for it," Sidney said. "I mean, there's no way I could. 'Cause I don't know what I might have turned out to be; it's just one of those things." Now, as a teenager, Sidney wondered whether the assaults had steered his life toward homosexuality. "I mean, I'm happy the way I am, too," he said, "but I'd like to have seen what would have happened if that wouldn't have happened. 'Cause I don't know if this is the way I would have turned out or not." In Sidney's case his environment, rather than genetics or biology, probably had the greatest influence on his decision to accept homosexuality.

Jeffrey, a gay teenager interviewed in 2000 by the *New York Times Magazine*, experienced quite a different environment when, at the age of 15, he realized he was gay. Jeffrey grew up in a conservative community in the South and attended a Baptist church where the minister often condemned homosexuality. Jeffrey knew no homosexuals in high school, and he told the magazine that his family expected him to marry a Christian girl, settle down, and raise a lot of children. And yet, despite the lack of gay influences in his environment, Jeffrey found himself attracted to boys. "I'm a Christian—I'm like, how could God possibly do this to me?" Jeffrey told the magazine. Unlike Sidney, in Jeffrey's case it could be argued that environment had virtually nothing to do with his decision to accept homosexuality.

For decades, the cause of homosexuality was attributed to ***psychiatric*** factors, and many psychiatrists believed that homosexuality was a mental illness. Therefore, since homosexuals were sick, psychiatrists thought they could cure them. During the 1940s, some gay men were lobotomized—a radical surgery that includes slicing away sections of the brain. Evidently, doctors believed they could chop out the part of the brain that made a person gay. Another technique tried on gay men was electroshock therapy. In some cases, doctors thought they could rid men of their homosexual tendencies by zapping their brains with electricity.

Some psychiatrists tried aversion therapy. In Canada, *Toronto Star* reporter David Graham recalled that in the early 1970s, while attending college, he sought to be cured of his homosexuality at a psychiatric hospital. His physician attached electrodes to his ankles and wrists, then made Graham watch slide projections of photographs depicting homosexual acts. Whenever Graham saw a slide, he would receive a painful jolt of electricity. "With each stimulating vision came an abrupt, teeth-numbing shock," Graham wrote years later. "It was a crude form of aversion therapy and I was an enthusiastic patient. Just out of my teens, the prospect of a life as a homosexual seemed unthinkably depressing." In Graham's case, the aversion therapy failed. He accepted his homosexuality and got on with his life.

Women seeking the "cure" submitted to radical surgeries as well—it was believed that a **hysterectomy** could cure lesbianism. Other lesbians were injected with the female hormone **estrogen** under the belief, perhaps, that their bodies were not producing enough of the chemical on their own and that is why they were acting like men. In the end, none of these treatments worked. While doing the research for his 1947 book *Sexual Behavior in the Human Male*, Dr. Alfred Kinsey interviewed many "former" homosexuals who claimed to have been cured. Instead, Kinsey reported that what he found were homosexuals who were suppressing their homosexuality.

In 1974 the American Psychiatric Association voted to remove homosexuality from its list of mental illnesses—and that decision was hardly unanimous. Nearly 40 percent of the association's membership voted in favor of keeping it on the list and some mental health professionals still believe they can cure homosexuality. In 1992, New York City psychiatrist Charles Socarides told *Newsweek* that he maintains a busy practice turning troubled gay people into "happy, fulfilled heterosexuals." For the most part, though, psychiatrists treat their gay patients by counseling them to accept their homosexuality and helping them feel comfortable with their lifestyles.

Common Genetic Bonds

Once doctors stopped thinking of homosexuality in terms of mental illness, they turned their attention to *physiological* causes. By the time Simon LaVay started studying the brains of human cadavers, other scientists had spent years laying the groundwork for his discovery and for others. For decades, it had been believed that there were no differences between male and female brains. Starting in the 1970s, several studies showed that there are, in fact, physical differences, and those differences cause men and women to act in different ways. Their brains control aggression and sex drive, how they eat, and how they nurture their young, among other activities. Some of the studies concentrated on the hypothalamus—the part of the brain that regulates a number of bodily functions, including sexual activity. In 1977, University of California at Los Angeles neurobiologist Roger Gorski determined that the hypothalamus in a male rat is five times larger than in a female. Gorski's research posed a new question: if the hypothalamus is different in men and women, would similar differences

show up when the brains of homosexuals and heterosexuals are compared?

That is the question LaVay sought to answer when he commenced the study at the Salk Institute. LaVay and his team dissected the brains of 41 male and female cadavers, including 19 homosexual men who had died from Acquired Immune Deficiency Syndrome (AIDS). In each case they looked at the hypothalamus, which is the size of a snowflake. In all but a few of the cases, LaVay found that the hypothalamuses in women and gay men were less than half the size as those found in heterosexual men. Therefore, they concluded that gay men are born with a physical trait that makes them different from straight men.

LaVay cautioned, though, that his research did not provide overwhelming support that homosexuality could be traced to a tiny section of the brain. For example, his study did not address homosexuality among women — he was unable to find cadavers of admitted gay women. And LaVay also subscribed to the argument that biology could only partly answer the question of why people choose to be gay. "What I reported was a difference in the brain structure of the hypothalamus," LaVay told *Newsweek*. "We can't say on the basis of that what makes people gay or straight. But it opens the door to find the answer to that question."

LaVay released the results of his tests as another groundbreaking study into the cause of homosexuality was completed. That study was performed by psychologist Michael Bailey of Northwestern University and psychiatrist Richard Pillard of Boston University School of Medicine. The Bailey-Pillard study focused on sets of identical and fraternal twins, and concluded that if one identical twin is gay, the other is nearly three times more likely to be gay than if the twins are fraternal. Identical twins share a more common genetic bond than fraternal twins. The study also showed that if one identical twin is gay, his twin sibling is five times more likely to be gay than if the two are adoptive brothers, who share no genetic bonds at all. The Bailey-Pillard study provided substantial evidence suggesting that homosexuality is linked through genetics.

Critics were quick to question the results of the LaVay and Bailey-Pillard studies. For starters, critics argued, neither study tried to find a biological reason for lesbianism. Also, the Bailey-Pillard study was criticized because it analyzed twins who had grown up together and, therefore, had been exposed to similar influences and environments. Surely, if one twin was affected by his environment, most likely the other twin would be exposed to the same influences as well. On the other hand, many people welcomed the news that the cause of homosexuality might be biological and inherited. Among the people embracing the scientific developments were the parents of gays, many of whom had been blaming themselves for their children's lifestyle choices. Mothers and fathers who thought they had failed as parents suddenly realized that regardless of what type of parents they had been, they could never have influenced their children's sexual preferences.

The X Chromosome

The LaVay research studied the size of a component of the brain. The Bailey-Pillard research was based primarily on interviews with twins. Dr. Dean Hamer, working at the National Cancer Institute in Bethesda, Maryland, took the research a step further. Hamer studied actual genetic material and concluded that a group of genes sitting at one end of a *chromosome* identified as Xq28 were similar in 33 pairs of 40 gay brothers who contributed DNA to the experiment. Hamer did not discover the "gay gene" — the one gene that theoretically links all gay men — but merely identified the place where, after further research, it might be found. Still, Hamer's work was heralded as a significant step forward in providing definitive proof that gay people inherit homosexuality from their ancestors. In the case of Xq28, Hamer's research suggested that gay men inherit homosexuality from their mothers. Xq28 is a so-called "X" chromosome, which men inherit from their mothers. "When we collected the family histories, we saw more gay relatives on the maternal side than on the paternal side," Hamer said in an interview with *Science* magazine.

Once again, science had added weight to the theory that homosexuality is "a naturally occurring and common variation," according to Peri Jude Radecic, a spokesperson for the National Gay and Lesbian Task Force interviewed by *USA Today*. But when the Hamer results were announced, some gay activists found new reasons to be concerned. If a gay gene is eventually isolated, they worried that science would also find a way to eliminate it. After all, one of the predicted outcomes of so-called **stem cell** research is to isolate and eliminate genes in people who carry Alzheimer's disease and other illnesses passed down from generation to generation. One might argue that if the Alzheimer's gene can eventually be eliminated, so too could a gay gene be eliminated. Gay playwright Jonathan Tolin told *USA Today*, "Are people going to say 'Hey, this is great' or are they going to say, 'Well, we've found the cause of this terrible thing and now we should try to cure it?'"

Thus, when young gay people ask themselves why they are gay, the answer could come from any number of places: the home in which they grew up, or in the DNA found in a lock of their hair, or in a snowflake-sized component of their brains, pulsing deep inside their skulls. Or, it might come from all those places.

Chapter Three

Depression is a common, and unfortunate, reality for many young gays, because they often feel alienated from their peers.

Plagues on the Young Gay Community

Jim Wheeler grew up in Lebanon, Pennsylvania, a small town where most residents observe conservative Christian values. A lot of the people who knew Jim were unsure what to make of him, because he was different from many other young men in the town. Jim was an accomplished artist and poet who wore flamboyant clothes, had his tongue pierced, and made friends mostly with girls. When Jim was a junior in high school, he told his parents he was gay. They were not surprised.

When Jim was in high school, he was constantly bullied and harassed. Even after graduation, he suffered from depression brought on by his classmates' cruelty. After high school Jim left Lebanon briefly to enroll in art school in Philadelphia, but he was not happy there and returned home. He moved into an apartment above his father's medical office.

"Jim was on a crash course," his mother, Susan Wheeler, told a reporter for the *Harrisburg Patriot-News*. "He had the support of his family, but he needed more than that. He had no peer group." A few months after Jim Wheeler moved back to Lebanon, he committed suicide, alone, in his apartment. He was 19 years old. Jim left behind the poems he had written, many of them telling the story of what it is like for a young gay person in the United States. Here is an excerpt from one of his poems, titled "Jim in Bold":

... Thinking contemplating wishing dreaming

Screaming hissing living loving hugging kissing Yelling

Crying dying listening hearing touching smelling tasting

Seeing believing missing myself until i receive a divine

message maybe from somewhere way up above and if i believe

in the christian god then id say that god spoke to me telling me it's better

to be Hated for what you

are then loved for what youre not ...

"[Being] a young gay boy growing up in a religious area can lead to self-loathing and guilt," Susan Wheeler told the *Patriot-News*. "I always thought Christ was very accepting and loving to all kinds of people. [Homosexuals] are who they are, it's genetic, they don't choose. Homophobia must be overcome through education."

Jim Wheeler's life ended the way the lives of many young gay people end: in suicide. Over the years, numerous studies have shown that young gay people attempt suicide at rates much higher than heterosexuals. And although some recent studies have questioned those statistics—suggesting that suicide rates among young gays are not significantly higher than the rates among heterosexual youths—there is no question that young gay people find themselves facing depression and other factors that lead to risky behavior. In a statement presented to a U.S. Senate committee in 2004, the American Academy of Child and Adolescent Psychiatry and the American Psychiatric Association said:

There is strong evidence that gay, lesbian and bisexual youth of both sexes are significantly more likely to experience suicidal thoughts and attempted suicide. A number of studies have shown that the increased risk ranges from two-fold to seven-fold. Gay, lesbian and bisexual youths were shown in these studies to carry a number of risk factors for suicidal behavior, including high rates of drug and alcohol use. Gay adolescents are at significant risk for suicide due to chronic bullying and victimization at school.

Depression. Suicide. Drug and alcohol abuse. Those are not the only problems many young gay people find themselves facing. Some gay teenagers also practice unsafe sex. That means they are at risk to contract AIDS, a potentially fatal sexually transmitted disease.

Knowing How Lonely It Can Be

A study conducted in 1989 by the U.S. Alcohol, Drug Abuse and Mental Health Administration titled *Gay Male and Lesbian Youth Suicide* reported a high suicide rate among gay teens, finding that young gay and lesbian people are confused and traumatized by society's attitudes toward homosexuality. The study said gay and lesbian youth are strongly affected by the negative attitudes and hostile responses of society to homosexuality. According to the study, young gays experience poor self-esteem, depression, and fear. Also, the report said, gay and lesbian youth are often driven to suicidal behavior due to the ongoing discrimination against gays as well as society's portrayal of homosexuals as self-destructive. The author, Paul Gibson, wrote, "Gay and lesbian youth take tremendous risks by being open about who they are. You have to respect their courage . . . Openly homosexual youth are an affront to a society that would like to believe they don't exist. Our culture seems to have particular disdain for those gay youth who do not conform to gender expectations."

Since then, a number of studies have supported the notion that

gay teenagers attempt suicide at rates higher than heterosexual youths. One of the most recent studies was a 1998 report compiled by researchers at the University of Minnesota who questioned 394 gay or bisexual high school and middle school students as well as 336 heterosexual students. The researchers found that 28 percent of the gay or bisexual boys reported making at least one attempt to take their own lives, compared to just 4 percent of heterosexual boys. In other words, young gay boys had an attempted suicide rate seven times higher than the rate for heterosexual boys. The lead author of the study, pediatrician Gary Remafedi, told the *Minneapolis Star Tribune* that gay teens suffer from a "social stigma." He said, "Boys who are considered more feminine are subject to maltreatment" by their peers.

It should be pointed out, though, that the Minnesota study found the suicide attempt rate among gay girls was not much higher than the rate for heterosexual girls. What's more, the authors of the Minnesota study noted that many suicide attempts don't come close to being lethal; therefore, it is often difficult to tell whether the actual suicide rate among gays is appreciably higher than the rate among heterosexual youths. "Death certificates generally do not reflect the sexual orientation of the deceased, and the sexual orientation of suicide victims is difficult to ascertain posthumously,"

Remafedi and the other authors wrote in an article published in the *American Journal of Public Health*.

One critic of the Minnesota study was Cornell University psychologist Ritch Savin-Williams, who argued that young gays do not always tell the truth on questionnaires. In 2001, Savin-Williams released the results of his own study of 349 high school and college students between the ages of 17 and 25. Savin-Williams found that while many gay students claimed to have made attempts to take their own lives, what more than half of the respondents really meant was that they were "thinking about" committing suicide. "They're trying to communicate that they do have difficult lives," Savin-Williams told *USA Today*. "But most gay kids are healthy and resilient."

The truth probably falls somewhere between what Remafedi found and the scenario suggested by Savin-Williams. While it is true that most gay teens are able to handle the stress, some are unable to cope. It does not shock gay teens to learn their friends have made attempts to take their own lives, usually after suffering from depression for months or years. Ryan Wallace, a gay teen from Utah, told *Rolling Stone* in 1998 that he tried to kill himself at the age of 14 by slashing his wrists with a razor blade. Ryan told the magazine that he was driven to making a suicide attempt because he was intensely lonely and had no one to turn to for support. Ironically, the *Rolling Stone* reporter encountered Ryan while interviewing young people who had been friends with a gay Utah teen named Jacob Orosco, who had just killed himself.

Another gay teenager, Emaleigh Ardron Doley, wrote in an essay in the *Advocate*, "I know first-hand how lonely it can be if you're 'different.' . . . It's hard, but I'm not going to change—I like who I am. During my junior year I struggled with depression. I

was able to overcome it because I decided that society was not going to shove me way back in the closet and lock the door. I've seen so many other kids who are questioning their sexuality and beating themselves up because they think they don't have anywhere to turn."

There is no question, though, that depressed gay youths often seek relief in the same places other depressed people seek relief—through alcohol and drugs. According to the New York-based Sexuality Information and Education Council of the United States, a 1995 study conducted by health officials in Massachusetts found that "gay, lesbian and bisexual orientation was associated with an increased lifetime frequency of use of cocaine, crack, anabolic steroids, inhalants, 'illegal' and injectable drugs. Gay, lesbian and bisexual youth were more likely to report using tobacco, marijuana and cocaine before 13 years of age."

Regardless of sexual preference, thoughts of suicide are common among American young people, according to the Gallup Youth Survey. A 2003 poll asked 1,200 young people between the ages of 13 and 17, "Do you personally know any teenagers who have tried to commit suicide?" A total of 47 percent of the respondents answered "yes." What's more, 37 percent of the young people who participated in the survey said they had discussed suicide with their friends, 25 percent admitted that they had entertained thoughts of committing suicide themselves, 9 percent said they had "come close" to attempting suicide, and 7 percent said they actually took a step toward committing the act.

Making the Wrong Choice

Gay teens who can handle the mental stress of being homosexual in a straight world face other risks. Consider the case of Peter "Pedro" Zamora, who emigrated to America at the age of eight, a passenger aboard a leaky boat that sailed from Cuba to Florida. Pedro's family arrived in America with little else except the clothes they were wearing. As a young boy Pedro could speak no English, yet there is no question that he possessed a keen intelligence. Pedro was also a good athlete and a natural leader. At Hialeah Junior High School in Miami, Pedro was president of the Science Club and captain of the cross-country team. His classmates voted him "most intellectual" boy and "best all-around student." Everyone in Pedro's family expected him to do great things—to go to college and eventually become a doctor, lawyer, or corporate executive. Pedro was also gay, a fact that did not seem to get in the way of what he intended to accomplish in life.

Pedro told a reporter for the *Wall Street Journal* that he recalled a doctor speaking to his seventh-grade class about a disease known as AIDS. It was the mid-1980s, when the AIDS epidemic had reached its peak, killing some 62,000 victims, mostly homosexual men who practiced sex without condoms. "A doctor came to talk to our class," Pedro told the *Wall Street Journal*. "He wore a

three-piece suit and had gray hair and was talking about AIDS
. . . His attitude was that we know you will never need this information because you aren't sexually active, but we're giving it to
you anyway. He didn't talk about sex practices. He didn't talk
about condoms. He didn't talk about testing."

Soon Pedro would become *promiscuous*, having sex with several other homosexual friends but never using the protection of a
condom. In 1989, Pedro participated in a school blood drive. A
short time later, he received a letter from the American Red Cross
advising him there was a "problem" with the blood he donated. At
first Pedro ignored the Red Cross letter as well as several other letters from the organization. Finally, he went to see his family doctor, where a blood test revealed that he had tested positive for
human immunodeficiency virus, or HIV, the virus that causes
AIDS. He was 17 years old.

At first, Pedro was devastated by the news. But perhaps knowing that he did not have long to live, Pedro soon collected himself
and became a tireless promoter of AIDS education in the United
States. He visited high schools, warning students that AIDS can be
spread through both heterosexual and homosexual sex, and warning them to use condoms if they chose to have sex. Eventually,
Pedro became a nationally known figure when he was selected for
a role on MTV's *The Real World*, living in a home in San Francisco
with several other young people whose lives were chronicled by
the reality TV show. On the show, Pedro played himself—an openly gay young person. He was featured on magazine covers and
appeared on network news magazines and talk shows. He also
testified before Congress, hoping to convince lawmakers to
approve more funding for AIDS education in the United States.
Perhaps recalling his own experience with the aloof physician who

spoke to his seventh-grade class, Pedro told members of Congress, "If you want to reach me as a young gay man, especially a young gay man of color, then you need to give me information in a language and vocabulary I can understand and relate to."

By the time the last episodes of *The Real World* were filmed in June 1994, Pedro was still healthy and actively spreading his message about AIDS. But then, suddenly, he grew ill and he died that November. "That's where the real tragedy, the real mystery of the disease lies," MTV executive Doug Herzog told the *Buffalo News*. "He leaves the house a healthy man, or seemingly healthy. Four short months later, we're saying our goodbyes to him."

Pedro Zamora, a young gay Cuban American, was infected with the AIDS virus when he was 17 years old. His story attracted national attention and sympathy after he was chosen as a cast member for the MTV program *The Real World*. Until his death in 1994, Zamora often spoke to groups of young people in order to raise awareness of AIDS.

Today, there is still no cure for AIDS, nor is there a vaccine that would prevent people from catching the disease. There are drugs that have been found to be effective in combating it in the body, either slowing down its effects or virtually (but not completely) eradicating the virus from the body of the patient. Because of those advancements, as well as greater public awareness of the disease, the number of AIDS-related deaths in the United States has fallen since the mid-1990s. But young people are still afflicted with the disease, and the victims include many homosexual youths.

Several studies confirm that young gay people are at risk. In 1998, the U.S. Centers for Disease Control and Prevention (CDC) reported that AIDS is the sixth-leading cause of death among young people between the ages of 15 and 24. "Unprotected sexual intercourse and multiple sex partners place young persons at risk for HIV infection," the agency reported. In 2000, the CDC said nearly 1,700 people between the ages of 13 and 24 were afflicted with AIDS, and nearly half of those infected were homosexual boys and men. Those numbers indicate gays make up a disproportionate number of AIDS victims, given the fact that even by Dr. Alfred Kinsey's estimate, gay people make up no more than 10 percent of the population.

In 1996, the *American Journal of Public Health* published a report stating that 43 percent of young gay and bisexual men who participated in the study admitted to having unprotected sex during a six-month period covered by the study. Also that year, the county of Contra Costa in California issued an *HIV/AIDS Epidemiology Report* stating that 240 individuals with AIDS in the county were likely to have been infected as teenagers. "At first, I tried to blame it on the person who I think gave it to me, but I realized it was really my fault for not making him put on a condom," a 15-year-old AIDS patient named Jason told the *Contra Costa Times*. "He gave me the choice of which way to do it, and I made the wrong one. I was so stupid, and now I have to pay for it."

According to the Gallup Youth Survey, AIDS remains a major concern among young people. A 2003 Gallup Youth Survey asked 1,200 teens between the ages of 13 and 17 to list the most urgent health problems facing America. Twenty-four percent of the respondents named AIDS as the country's most urgent health concern, giving the disease top status over cancer (18 percent), obesity (11 percent), and heart disease (2 percent). What's more, in a poll of 785 young people conducted in 2004, teens were asked this question: "How concerned are you that you, yourself, will get AIDS—very concerned, a little concerned, not very concerned or not at all concerned?" Eleven percent of the respondents said they are "very concerned" while 18 percent said they are "a little concerned." The remaining respondents said they had few worries about contracting the disease. Nevertheless, nearly a third of the young people who responded to the poll did express some concern that they would be exposed to AIDS. The Gallup Youth Survey also asked teens whether they believe AIDS is a serious problem among their friends. Forty-four percent of the respondents said AIDS is a "very serious" problem, while 16 percent said they believe the disease is a "somewhat serious" problem.

Hope and Support

AIDS, depression, drug and alcohol abuse, and suicide represent great threats to the lives of young gay people. The pressures that society places on young gays were illustrated in a 2003 documentary film about Jim Wheeler, titled *Jim in Bold*. The film was shown on PBS stations and on MTV and was featured at several gay and lesbian film festivals. The filmmakers wanted to do more

How concerned are you that you will get AIDS?

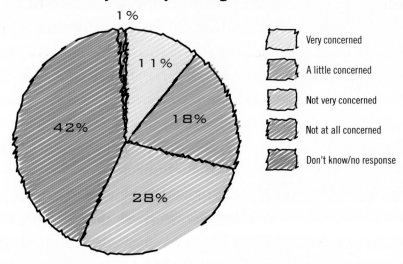

1%
11%
18%
42%
28%

Very concerned

A little concerned

Not very concerned

Not at all concerned

Don't know/no response

Poll taken January–March 2004; 785 total respondents age 13–17.
Source: The Gallup Organization

How serious a problem do you think AIDS is among your teenaged friends?

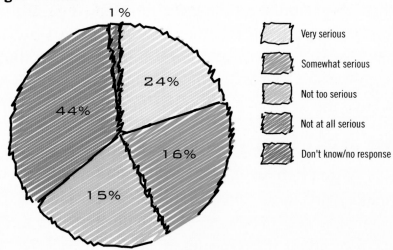

1%
24%
44%
16%
15%

Very serious

Somewhat serious

Not too serious

Not at all serious

Don't know/no response

Poll taken August 2003; 517 total respondents age 13–17.
Source: Gallup Youth Survey/The Gallup Organization

than just tell Jim Wheeler's story; they wanted to show what it is truly like to be a gay teenager living in the United States.

Despite the sad ending to Jim Wheeler's life, the film is largely upbeat, showing other young gays that there is hope and support for them. To produce the documentary, the filmmakers gave a camera to two young gay men and sent them on a journey across the country, interviewing other young gays. Director Glenn Holstein told the *Austin Chronicle*, "I joined them in New Jersey for one of the final interviews at a high school where there's a [Gay-Straight Alliance], and that was shocking to me because I'm a 40-year-old man, and it's been a while since I was in high school. When I was in high school, terms like 'gay' and 'queer' and 'fag' were barbs that were shot at me in the hallways. And here were kids talking in an incredibly supportive way with each other, both gay and straight, using terms that they were comfortable with, and that was a big surprise to me."

As for Jim's former high school, five years after he took his own life the place where he endured years of abuse has a decidedly different attitude toward gays. The high school started a support group for gay teens, and by 2003 the organization had a membership of 10 students. One student told the *Patriot-News*, "When Jim was here, there were probably gay teens but they didn't come out because they were afraid." Jim Wheeler's former high school changed in the five years since he took his own life, and other high schools have also come to realize the importance of recognizing that gay teens have rights. Sadly, some high schools have not.

Chapter Four

Two gay students speak to reporters after winning a court ruling that allowed them to attend their school's prom together. While incidents of gay students attending the prom together have become more common, some homosexual teens choose instead to hold their own proms.

High School Years: Harassment, Abuse, and Hope

llen Wolff, a 17-year-old student at Baker High School in Syracuse, New York, wore a black tuxedo with a silver vest to his senior prom. His date was Misko Lencek-Inagaki, who also wore a black tuxedo. "We danced, ate chocolate-covered strawberries, chocolate chip cannolis, and drank lots and lots of soda," Allen told a reporter for MSNBC. Allen said his prom was, simply, "Absolutely amazing."

Adriyn Hayes chose not to wear a taffeta gown to her prom. Instead, she wore slacks and a jacket. But her date, Sophia Lanza-Weil, did wear a gown. "She wore a suit but I wanted to wear a dress," Sophia told MSNBC. "We've been dating for over a year. So I don't think it was a big shock to anyone that we walked through the door . . . We actually had a very good time."

Each year, thousands of high school seniors look forward to their proms. For many students, the prom may be one of the final times in which they can enjoy each other's company before they graduate, leave home for college or the armed forces, or find full-time jobs. For all seniors who go to their proms, the events are also celebrations that mark the final days of their high school years.

For years, young gay people found themselves left out of the celebrations. They either chose to stay home or, if they did go to their proms, they brought dates of the opposite sex. If a gay boy asked a girl to attend the prom with him he could join in the party, but deep down inside he may have felt awkward, uncomfortable, and out of place. In the book *Kings and Queens: Queers at the Prom*, South Carolina student Reid Davis told author David Boyer that at his prom in 1984 he escorted a girl named Kim while his friend Tim also brought a female date. "We danced," Reid said, "and I remember there was one song where the boys and the girls were dancing separately from each other—it was like a Kool and the Gang song, probably 'Celebration,' and the whole time I was thinking about Tim and that we were getting away with dancing together."

Today, many gay teens are far more comfortable with who they are, and their friends also accept them for who they are. As the cases of Allen Wolff, Misko Lencek-Inagaki, Adriyn Hayes, and Sophia Lanza-Weil prove, many young gay people are perfectly at ease with escorting same-sex dates to their proms. High school administrators have also learned to accept gays—albeit in many cases their acceptance has been driven by court orders upholding the rights of gay students to participate in school activities that were closed to them because of their sexual preferences. The senior prom is, in fact, a good example of one high school institution that was opened to gay participation with the help of a federal court order. In 1980, a gay student named Aaron Fricke sought permission to escort a boy named Paul to his high school prom in

Rhode Island. School officials turned him down, but ultimately a federal judge intervened, ruling that gay students cannot be denied admission to their proms.

Still, some school districts have been slow to respond. Until 2004, the Lago Vista School District in Texas prohibited students from buying prom tickets for same-sex dates, but dropped the policy after the civil rights group People for the American Way threatened to file a lawsuit. And in Utah, the American Civil Liberties Union threatened to sue a school district in a suburb of Salt Lake City for also prohibiting gay couples at the senior prom.

Despite their legal protection, many gay students still feel uncomfortable attending a party that has traditionally been intended for heterosexual couples. And so, some gay students choose to hold their own proms. "A prom is typically a highly heterosexual event, and the kids don't feel comfortable in that environment," Ilse Stoll Zinnes told the *Easton Express-Times* in Pennsylvania. Stoll Zinnes is the founder of HAVEN Youth Group, which in 2004 organized a gay-only prom in the Easton area. (HAVEN stands for Hope, Acceptance, Validation, Equality and Nurturing.)

Other than the fact that only gays attended, there was not much about Haven's "Prizm Prom" that was different than any of the thousands of other proms held across America in the spring of 2004. Students dressed up, paid $40 per couple for tickets, posed in their gowns and tuxedos for pictures shot by a professional photographer, and danced until midnight in a hotel ballroom. "Unfortunately, many queer youth have missed their high school proms for fear of harassment or ridicule, or they have felt the need to remain closeted in order to attend these gala events," HAVEN organizer Constance Kristofik told the *Express-Times*.

Attempting to Become Invisible

Anybody who has walked the hallways of a U.S. high school and witnessed the abuse, harassment, and humiliation heaped on gay students should not be shocked that many gay students are still hesitant to let their classmates know the truth about themselves. Even with court orders protecting their rights, many gay students continue to find themselves bullied and assaulted by classmates who harbor prejudices toward them. The experiences suffered by Derek Henkle are typical. As a high school sophomore in Nevada, Derek appeared on a local cable access TV show to talk about what life is like for gay students. Soon, students at his school started calling him "fag," "fairy," and "homo." One day, some students threw a rope around his neck and threatened to drag him behind a truck. Derek escaped to another classroom and called the school office to report that his life was in danger. A vice principal took two hours to show up, and then she greeted the incident with laughter. No action was taken against the students who assaulted him.

The harassment continued. Finally, Derek sought a transfer to another school, but the abuse continued there. He was cornered by a mob of students. One of the students stepped out of the mob and punched him in the face—an act that was witnessed by campus security. After the incident, the school security officers discouraged him from reporting the assault to the city police.

Derek eventually sued the school district for violating his First Amendment rights to free expression. In 2002, the school district agreed to pay Derek a settlement of $451,000 and revise its harassment policy, recognizing a student's right to disclose his sexual orientation. In addition, the school district also agreed to provide sensitivity training for teachers and administrators so that they would understand the problems of gay students and the issues they face in school.

For Derek Henkle, the settlement represented a hard-fought victory for a student forced to endure abuse at the hands of his classmates while school administrators stood by and did nothing. Not all gay students possess Derek's courage. In 2001, the civil rights group Human Rights Watch issued a report titled *Hatred in the Hallways: Violence and Discrimination Against Lesbian, Gay and Transgender Students in U.S. Schools*. The report found gay students enduring harassment and physical assaults at schools throughout

Students who are gay—or even those incorrectly believed to be homosexual—may find themselves the victim of jokes and humiliation from their peers.

the United States. Many gay students told the Human Rights Watch researchers that they believe their lives are in danger. Said the report:

> Lesbian, gay, bisexual, and transgender youth of school age in the United States often suffer daily harassment, abuse, and violence at the hands of their peers. These students spend an inordinate amount of energy figuring out how to get to and from school safely, avoiding the hallways when other students are present in order to escape slurs and shoves, cutting gym classes to escape being beaten up—in short, attempting to become invisible. For some, the burden of coping each day with relentless harassment is too much. They drop out of school. Some commit suicide. Others barely survive. A few fight back, demanding that school administrators ensure their safety, that recognition of gays and lesbians be integrated into the curriculum, that they be allowed to organize gay-straight student groups, and that they be encouraged to celebrate their identities.

The Gallup Youth Survey has confirmed that gay students face physical danger in their school hallways. A Gallup Youth Survey that polled 403 teenagers in 1999 asked young people who were aware of the existence of violent groups in their schools to identify the people most likely to be targeted. A total of 58 percent of the respondents said that violent groups of students in their schools target gays. Sixty-eight percent said members of those groups have assaulted students as well as teachers and other staff members. When the Gallup Youth Survey asked young people what subject members of violent youth groups talk about, 50 percent of the respondents answered, "hatred of gays."

One gay student who fought back was Jamie Nabozny. As a ninth-grader in Ashland, Wisconsin, Jamie endured taunts, shoves and physical assaults leveled at him by classmates. One morning, in a school bathroom, two boys confronted Jamie. "One pushed his knees into the back of mine," Jamie told *People Weekly*. "I fell into the urinal, and another kid started peeing on me. I just remember sitting there, waiting for it to get over with."

What do members of potentially violent groups in your school talk about?

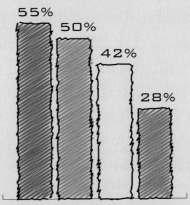

55%
50%
42%
28%

Satanism or devil workshop   Hatred of Gays

Hatred of Minorities   Admiration for Hitler and the Nazis

Who are the potential victims of violent groups in your school?

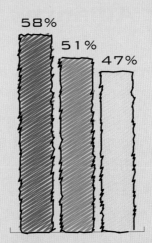

58%
51%
47%

 Gay Students   Minority Students   Every Student

Polls taken May 1999; 403 total teen respondents. Source: *Youthviews: The Newsletter of the Gallup Youth Survey*, October 1999/The Gallup Organization

For two years, the beatings and humiliations continued. Each time he was assaulted, Jamie and his parents complained to school administrators—who chose to do nothing. In the 11th grade, one of the assaults resulted in Jamie's hospitalization. Jamie decided he could take no more. He filed a federal lawsuit against the Ashland School District, and in 1996 a judge in Chicago ruled that the school district had the responsibility to protect him from the assaults. As a result of the lawsuit, the school district agreed to a $900,000 cash payment to Jamie. The Nabozny decision represented a landmark victory to gay students: for the first time, a court determined their civil rights had to be observed by public schools. Jamie told *People Weekly*, "This one kid in Texas came up to me and said, 'When I was in high school, I had the biggest picture of you on my locker. Every day the thing that got me through all of my classes was knowing you were going to be there.'"

Gay-Straight Alliances

In 1998, gay college student Matthew Shepard was kidnapped, tied to a fence, pistol-whipped, robbed, and left to die. The two killers each received sentences of life in prison for the murder. According to prosecutors, the killers were motivated both by robbery and hatred for gay people. The coldness of the Shepard murder and the insensitivity displayed by the killers shocked gay and straight students across the United States. Many of them resolved to make society a safer place for gays, particularly in their schools. Some did this by establishing Gay-Straight Alliances, or GSAs, in their high schools.

First established in 1988, GSAs were seen as support groups for gay students, but they were intended to be much more. Since straight students join as well, the clubs help show people in the school community that gay people do not have to face homophobia alone. Straight friends would be there for them. Following the Shepard murder, students worked together to form GSAs in hundreds of schools. According to the New York-based Gay Lesbian and Straight Education Network, which helps students form GSAs, more than 1,900 gay-straight student groups had been organized in American schools by late 2003.

A typical GSA can be found at Staples High School in Westport, Connecticut, where in 2000 one of the members was Jordan Heimer, a straight youth who was also captain of the school's wrestling team. In an interview with *Time*, Jordan said, "I help set the tone . . . Preaching doesn't work, but I try to use humor—or in the case of freshmen, bullying—to let them know how stupid they sound when they use words like faggot."

Not all schools have been receptive to the idea of establishing GSAs. At El Modena High School in Orange, California, 16-year-old gay student Anthony Colin filed a federal lawsuit against his school district because it turned down his request to form a GSA. Anthony told a reporter for *People Weekly* that he sought to organize the GSA because of the Shepard murder. "I've been harassed since kindergarten," Anthony told *People Weekly*. "For all I know, the next death might be me." To form the GSA, Anthony circulated a petition, gathering 500 signatures from the school's 1,900 students in support of the club. The petition eventually came before the school board, which rejected Anthony's request. Opponents of the GSA argued that students would use the meetings to discuss homosexual sex. "If you think the gay kids aren't seducing the other kids, you're nuts," opponent Donna Sigalas told *People Weekly*. Anthony next turned to the courts and filed his lawsuit. In the fall of 2000, the school board reached an out-of-court settlement with Anthony that permitted the El Modena High School Gay-Straight Alliance to meet.

Some public officials have gone to much greater lengths to discourage GSAs. In 1998, the Salt Lake City School Board in Utah found itself

confronted with a request by students to form a GSA at East High School. Under the federal Equal Access Act, which was passed by Congress in 1984, the school board members knew they could not prohibit the GSA while letting other extracurricular groups meet because that would have been a clear case of discrimination. So the school board developed a unique—and ultimately unsuccessful—strategy. Rather than permit the GSA, the board invoked a rule it had adopted in 1995 in response to a similar attempt to form a GSA: it banned all campus organizations "not directly related to curriculum" to "organize or meet on school property." That order not only prevented the East High School GSA from meeting in the school building, it dissolved dozens of other student organizations at all Salt Lake City schools. Such groups as the Black Student Union, the Latino Club, and the Native American Club were banned by the school board's order. Eventually, the strategy failed. The East High School GSA sued the Salt Lake City School Board, winning a federal court order permitting it to meet on campus.

In the classroom gays often find themselves fighting to be treated equally. Walk into any health class in an American high school, and chances are there will be scant information provided on health risks faced by gays and lesbians. At many high schools, when it comes to sex education the lesson plan is geared toward heterosexual conduct. "Sexuality education as it stands ignores gay youth, both lesbians and gay men," Heather Sawyer, a Chicago attorney for the gay civil rights group LAMBDA Legal Defense Fund, told the Web site Womensenews.org. "It renders them invisible, and by doing that you ignore particular health issues." In 1995, for example, the *Journal of Adolescent Health* reported that a Minnesota study showed lesbian and bisexual girls are more likely to become pregnant than heterosexual girls. "Youths that are struggling with their sexuality or sexual orientation are at risk for engaging in sexual behavior because they're trying to work things out," Sawyer told Womensenews.org.

According to LAMBDA, more than three-quarters of American health education teachers do not encourage class discussion about homosexuality and, in fact, one in twelve teachers tell their students that homosexuality is wrong. Even at schools where faculty members do teach gay health issues, there is a tendency to skim over the material. Edwin Neumann, a health education teacher in Levittown, Pennsylvania, told Womensenews.org, "Basically, we provide an explanation of what [homosexuality] is." He added that further discussion about gay issues—including the practice of safe sex, is "something that individual families make decisions on."

An Ideal World

One place where gay students do receive the health education they can use is Harvey Milk High School in New York. Named after slain San Francisco gay activist Harvey Milk, the school is one of the few gay-only educational institutions in America. Founded by the Hetrick-Martin Institute of New York,

Should teaching about homosexuality as an alternative lifestyle be required instruction, offered as an elective but not required, or not be taught at all?

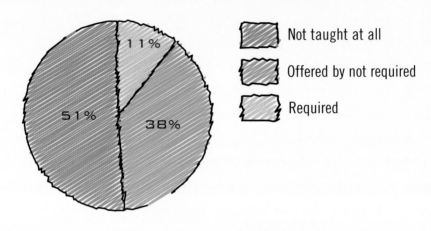

- Not taught at all
- Offered by not required
- Required

11%

51%

38%

Polls taken September–November 1999; 502 total teen respondents. Source: *Youthviews: The Newsletter of the Gallup Youth Survey*, April 2000/The Gallup Organization

the school started as a drop-in center for gay students who needed a safe haven from the harassment they were experiencing in their high schools. In 1984, the drop-in center expanded into a school and eventually, the tiny institution provided classes for about 50 students. In 2003, the New York City school system took over Harvey Milk High, provided it with a budget of more than $3 million, and opened its doors to nearly 200 gay and lesbian students. Harvey Milk valedictorian Dino Portalatin told *Attitude* magazine:

> When I was at a public school in Brooklyn, two of my closest friends outed me to the rest of the school. I got into fights just about every day from then on. School for me was terrifying. I'd run to class just as the bell rang to save myself. Often I didn't go to classes at all. One semester I had 85 absences, and when my mom saw the number '85' on my report she thought it was a grade for a class and congratulated me. I started to become really depressed

and began to feel I'd be better off dead than having to deal with constant harassment and fights. I started to see a counselor for my depression, and she recommended Harvey Milk. It made sense. I knew I wanted to do something with my life. I knew I had the potential and was a good kid, but it was all going to come to nothing if I kept on the way I was. I knew I wasn't going to make it in a mainstream high school.

Students at Harvey Milk go to classes, join clubs, and take part in extracurricular activities one would typically find at any U.S. high school. The difference is that at Harvey Milk, the students can do all those things without fear of harassment or abuse. (Occasionally, opponents of gay rights show up outside the school to protest as the students arrive in the morning or leave in the afternoon, but for the most part the students endure their taunts in stride, knowing they are safe inside Harvey Milk's doors.) "I think everybody feels that it's a good idea because some of the kids who are gays and lesbians have been constantly harassed and beaten in other schools," New York Mayor Michael Bloomberg told the Associated Press. "It lets them get an education without having to worry."

Elsewhere, gay-only high schools have struggled for acceptance. In Dallas, for example, Walt Whitman High School barely survives. The school has a tiny enrollment—students fill just five classrooms. Unlike Harvey Milk, Walt Whitman is a private school, meaning it operates without taxpayer assistance. The school was named after the gay poet Walt Whitman, whose poem *Salut au Monde* inspired the founders to establish the Dallas school. The poem contains these lines:

> Each of us inevitable;
> Each of us limitless—each of us with his or her right upon the earth.

In 2003, MTV aired a documentary on Walt Whitman High School, which helped call attention to the school's plight. Despite its handicaps, Walt Whitman fulfills its mission—to educate gay youths. In 2003, Walt Whitman Principal Becky Thompson told the *Advocate*, "It's difficult to sit in a classroom here and feel that educational needs are not being met. We've had kids who had spent their lives hiding at the back of classrooms and not learning, and that's not allowed here. We do a good job educating at Walt Whitman."

WHEN ATHLETES ARE GAY

The 1982 movie *Personal Best* told the story of two track stars who discover their lesbianism while training for the Olympics. In the film, one of the athletes is portrayed by Mariel Hemingway, who was 17 years old at the time she was cast for the role of Chris. The other lesbian character, Tory, was portrayed by Patrice Donnelly, a former Olympic athlete who is openly bisexual.

"I feel so proud to have played Tory," Donnelly told the *Advocate* in 1998. "In a way, she was the first realistic lesbian character ever on the screen. There were lesbians in movies before, but this was the first time that being lesbian didn't look like a disease. *Personal Best* showed us as good, wholesome, clean human beings who pursue excellence. It showed being a lesbian is not about deviance but about love."

Although *Personal Best* suggested that gays are as much a part of sports as anyone else, in reality few athletes have come out as homosexual. That is particularly true on the high school and college levels, most gay males are unwilling to disclose their homosexuality in the macho world of the training room. One who did was Dwight Slater, a 280-pound offensive lineman for Stanford University, who revealed his sexual orientation to his coach and then some of his teammates. In an interview with the *Advocate*, Slater said the coach and his teammates were clearly uncomfortable with his homosexuality; at the end of the season, he quit the team. "I was forced out of

The few gay students lucky enough to enroll in gay-only high schools are able to take advantage of educational opportunities that gays in many other U.S. high schools feel are denied them. However, segregating gay students from society may not be the right way to address the issue. It can be argued that schools would do well to provide better education to straight students, and their parents, about the rights of gay students. In a perfect world, gay students should be able to sit side-by-side with heterosexual students and not fear for their lives. But David Mensah, executive

football," Slater told the *Advocate* in 2002. "I will never forget how Coach seemed relieved when I told him I was leaving the team. He had my papers prepared for me to sign."

In 2001, gay activists made an effort to improve conditions for gay athletes in college. The San Francisco-based National Center for Lesbian Rights launched the Homophobia in Sport Project to advocate for the rights of gays to play college sports. "One of my concerns is that a lot of coaches and athletic directors are not willing to even consider that male sports athletes could be gay," Homophobia Project manager and former University of North Carolina girls' basketball coach Helen Carroll told the *Advocate*. "The mentality out there is a little like the military's: you simply can't be gay and play sports. These kids don't have any advocates. But I am guardedly optimistic because I think the top leadership of the [National Collegiate Athletic Association (NCAA)] gets the importance of the health and welfare of gay and lesbian athletes."

One of the Homophobia Project's recent accomplishments was assisting gay University of Florida softball player Andrea Zimbardi in her lawsuit against the university after she was kicked off the team. The case was settled too late for Andrea to be reinstated to the team—she had already graduated—but the university did agree to include sexual orientation in its nondiscrimination policy.

Several hundred people show their support for gays outside of Harvey Milk High School in New York. This photo was taken on the first day of school in 2003.

director of Harvey Milk, says that when it comes to relations between gay students and straight students, the world is hardly perfect. He told *Attitude*, "We all agree that it is important to move forward with efforts to ensure that our schools become safe and tolerant places for every student. In an ideal world the students we serve would be integrated into their local high school and there would be no need for us to exist. But until we achieve that goal, Harvey Milk is here for kids who need a safe place today."

Chapter Five

The stars of the television show *Queer Eye for the Straight Guy* attend the 2004 GLAAD (Gay and Lesbian Alliance Against Defamation) Media Awards. In recent years television shows like *Queer Eye* and *Will & Grace* have presented a positive view of homosexuals.

Struggling for Society's Acceptance

On March 15, 2004, millions of teenagers in the United States and Canada tuned in to the TV show *Degrassi: The Next Generation* to watch the long-awaited appearance of a character named Dylan. The show, versions of which have been filmed in Canada since 1982, depicts the lives of young people attending fictional Degrassi Community School in an urban Toronto neighborhood. Over the years, the show has tackled tough issues, such as drug use, depression, and date rape. The March 15, 2004, episode of *Degrassi* promised to continue that tradition with an examination of a gay relationship between two major characters.

Dylan, portrayed by 18-year-old actor John Bregar, is a tall, blond, athletic, hockey-playing boy. The other character featured in the episode, Marco, is portrayed by 17-year-old actor Adamo Ruggiero. Marco was not a new character—he had been featured before, including an episode in which he came out. Dylan was new to the series; his character was the often talked-about but never seen older brother of one of the Degrassi students. When Dylan finally made his appearance, it was to comfort Marco, who had just broken up with a girlfriend and was facing the fact that he could never have a straight relationship. As Marco sits by himself, staring pensively by a lakefront, Dylan approaches and puts his arm around the teenager. Next, they date. And then, they kiss. "The gay storyline is an example of the show's deft and thoughtful writing," wrote *Toronto Globe and Mail* television critic Andrew Ryan. "As per the *Degrassi* lineage, any morals or messages are handled honestly and without fanfare."

Degrassi is not the only show on TV to feature gay characters. In recent years, viewers have been treated to such programming in the mass media as *Queer Eye for the Straight Guy*, in which five gay men give tips on dressing, grooming, and style to heterosexual men preparing for dates with their girlfriends, and *Will & Grace*, a situation comedy featuring a gay character in the title role of Will Truman. What those shows prove is that gay people lead common and quite ordinary lives. "People grow up now with the idea of coming out and stuff like that," John Bregar said in an interview with the *Advocate*. "It's not such a surprise when they do. Our generation is growing up seeing it happen. People are opinionated, but seriously, bigger things happen."

In high school, gay students are often harassed, abused, and assaulted. But when they leave school, they often step into a much different world. Thirteen states and nearly 250 municipalities have laws on the books prohibiting discrimination on the basis of sexual preference. In states that do not specifically protect the rights of gays, authorities have used **anti-hate crime laws** to prosecute people who assault or otherwise commit crimes against gays. As a result, many young gay people are finding that society in general may be a bit more accepting of their lifestyles than they find in the hallways of their school buildings.

Young people in particular believe it may be time for gays to receive more respect in society. In 2003, the Gallup Youth Survey asked 1,200 teens between the ages of 13 and 17 whether they believe gays receive the right amount of respect in society. A total of 53 percent of the respondents said gays receive too little respect in society, while 25 percent said gays receive the right amount of respect and 21 percent said gays receive too much respect. By a wide margin, more girls than boys believe gay people do not receive enough respect in society. The Gallup Youth Survey said 66 percent of girls and 40 percent of boys believe gays receive too little respect. Overall, those numbers show that in the future, today's young people will be the force that drives society to become more accepting of gays.

Gay Literature Winning Awards

As the writers of *Degrassi* have proven, the entertainment media is prepared to examine the issue of teenage homosexuality with sensitivity and respect. Other teen-oriented TV shows that have examined gay issues include *Dawson's Creek, Felicity, Party of Five,* and *My So-Called Life.* All those shows featured gay characters in recurring roles. Other media have responded as well. In recent years, several novels aimed at the young gay market have been published, showing that book publishers realize gay readers are looking for literature they can relate to.

In 2001, the novels *Empress of the World* by Sara Ryan and *Rainbow Boys* by Alex Sanchez were published. Both books were written for the teenage market. In Ryan's book, two teenage girls meet at a summer camp for gifted children and fall in love. As for

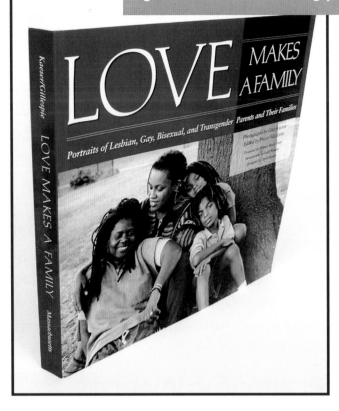

Sanchez' book, his story centers on three gay boys coming to terms with their sexuality. The characters include Nelson, an openly gay boy who is tormented in his high school; Jason, who has a girl-friend but is also an in-the-closet gay, and Kyle, who has a crush on Jason. Although not told in graphic detail, the book features sex between the characters. Sanchez told *USA Today*, "It is very hard to grow up feeling different," adding that he hoped his novel would help gay teens to be honest with themselves and say, "I am differ-ent, and I am not willing to hide that."

Librarians as well as educators welcome such books. Pat Scales, a spokesperson for the American Library Association, told *USA Today*, "I would rather have books that help them understand gay kids than shelter them . . . Libraries need to be about inclusion, not exclusion." Some of the other recent novels aimed at a gay teen audience include: *Annie on My Mind* and *The Year They Burned the Books* by Nancy Garden; *The Year of Ice: A Novel* by Brian Malloy; *Boy Meets Boy* by David Levithan; *Geography Club* by Brent Hartinger; and *Keeping You a Secret* by Julie Anne Peters. In a 2003 essay on teen-oriented gay literature for the on-line literary magazine Salon.com, writer Sarah Wildman said, "The sheer number of books that have come out in the last five years is an indicator of a sea change in the market. From 1969 until 1998 . . . 28 young-adult novels appeared with gay, lesbian or bisexual characters. From 1998 until [2003], 42 more novels have been published. The Gay, Lesbian and Straight Education Network . . . lists dozens of books recommended for teen readers, nearly all of which have been published in the last few years. And, in another sign these books are gaining mass acceptance, they are winning awards."

Indeed, many of the books do receive critical praise. The University of Illinois *Bulletin for the Center for Children's Books* said of *Boy Meets Boy*, "In a genre filled with darkness, torment and anxiety, it is a shiningly affirmative and hopeful book." *School Library Journal*, reviewing *Annie on My Mind*, said, "There have been many books for teenagers, fiction and nonfiction, that give lots of useful and accurate information about homosexuality; here's one that tells what it feels like, one that has, finally, romance." And *Publisher's Weekly*, which reviewed *The Year of Ice: A Novel*, said, "Malloy . . . handles the gay angle nicely as he explores Kevin's difficulty in finding an outlet for his hormonal urges even as he struggles to maintain a relationship with a classmate named Allison Minczeski, who falls for him. The author also displays a razor-sharp comic touch in the verbal sparring between father and son." In an interview with the *Advocate*, 38-year-old *Geography Club* author Brent Hartinger said there are more novels written about gay teens now simply because society is more willing to discuss the issue in an open and frank way. "People my age could often leave [homosexuality] unsaid," he commented. "Now it's all said."

A "Right" to Exclude Gays

There are still people and institutions in society that are uncomfortable with homosexuality. In 2003, for example, Republican U.S. Senator Rick Santorum of Pennsylvania inflamed gay rights activists when he suggested in a news interview that homosexuality is "antithetical to strong, healthy families," adding, "If . . . you have the right to consensual [gay] sex within your home, then you have the right to *bigamy*, you have the right to *polygamy*, you have the right to *incest*, you have the right to *adultery*. You have the right to anything. Does that undermine the fabric of our society? I would argue yes, it does."

Santorum was quickly criticized by many gay rights activists as well as political leaders for his remarks, which they regarded as insensitive and not part of mainstream thinking in the United States. Said Republican Senator Olympia Snowe of Maine, "Discrimination and bigotry have no place in our society, and I believe Senator Santorum's unfortunate remarks undermine Republican principles of inclusion and opportunity." Even so, many organizations rallied to Santorum's defense. The Christian Coalition, for one, released a statement calling the senator a "man of honor." Christian Coalition President Roberta Combs told CNN, "Homosexuality clearly is an alternative lifestyle. We stand with and support Senator Santorum."

One very large group that remains closed to gay participants is the Boy Scouts of America (BSA). In fact, the Scouts have taken aggressive efforts to keep gay Scouts and adult Scout leaders out of their ranks, which number some 3 million boys and teenagers.

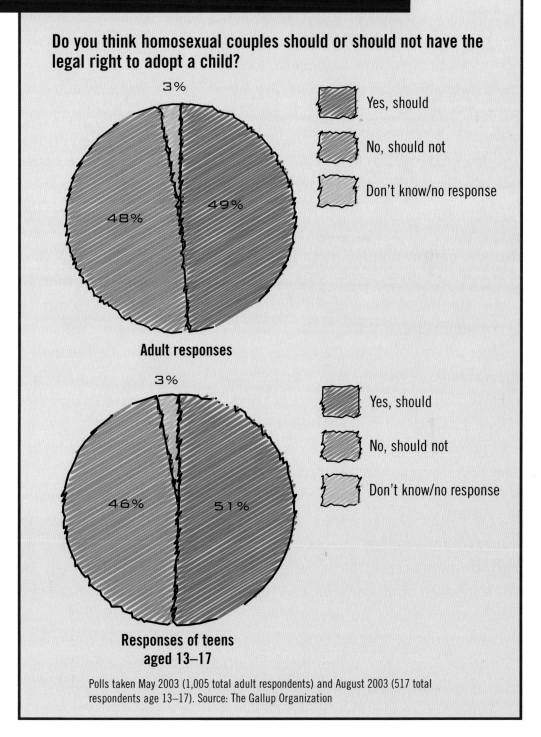

Do you think homosexual couples should or should not have the legal right to adopt a child?

Adult responses

3%

48%

49%

Yes, should

No, should not

Don't know/no response

Responses of teens aged 13–17

3%

46%

51%

Yes, should

No, should not

Don't know/no response

Polls taken May 2003 (1,005 total adult respondents) and August 2003 (517 total respondents age 13–17). Source: The Gallup Organization

In 2000, a court case brought by a former Eagle Scout reached the U.S. Supreme Court, which ruled in a narrow 5–4 decision that the BSA does have a right to exclude gays.

BSA is one of the largest organizations of young people in the United States. Boys who join learn to appreciate the outdoors and conserve the environment. Scouts learn the techniques of camping and trailblazing, but they also learn much more, such as the benefits of volunteerism and how to be leaders. There is no question that the Boy Scouts do prepare young men to be leaders: half the members of the U.S. Congress were Boy Scouts, and so were dozens of astronauts, including Alan B. Shepard Jr., the first American to fly in space, and Neil A. Armstrong, the first man to walk on the moon. Gerald Ford was the first Eagle Scout to become president of the United States.

Every boy who joins the Scouts is required to learn a creed called the Scout Oath, which says, "On my honor I will do my best to do my duty to God and my country and to obey the Scout Law; to help other people at all times; to keep myself physically strong, mentally awake, and morally straight." It is the commitment to be "morally straight" that BSA leaders insist permits them the right to exclude gays.

The BSA has never accepted gays since the Scouts were established in the United States in 1910. Scout leaders turned away adult volunteers they suspected of being gay, believing them to be bad influences on the young members. The involvement of church-based and conservative groups with the Boy Scouts of America probably influenced the BSA's attitude toward gays, because most religious leaders condemn homosexuality as a sin. Congregations of all religious denominations—Christian, Jewish, Muslim, Buddhist, and others—sponsor of Boy Scout troops.

There have been other reasons for the BSA's reluctance to admit gay members, however. In 1974, the organization was rocked by a scandal when the leaders of a troop in New Orleans were arrested on child sex charges. The men had formed the troop in a tough, inner-city neighborhood in an apparently admirable effort to teach impoverished youths how to be Scouts. What they really had in mind, though, was to sexually abuse the Scouts. Police arrested the leaders, who were eventually sentenced to lengthy prison terms.

Over the years, the BSA had successfully resisted efforts by girls and *atheists* who filed lawsuits to gain entry to the Scouts. In 1991, the Boy Scouts of America released a statement that said, "We believe that homosexual conduct is inconsistent with the requirement in the Scout Oath that a Scout be morally straight and in the Scout Law that a Scout be clean in word and deed, and that homosexuals do not provide a desirable role model for Scouts."

Many people have protested the decision by the Boy Scouts of America to exclude gays from being part of the organization.

A Place to Belong

James Dale, a Boy Scout from Sandy Hook, New Jersey, had no reason to believe he did not fit the BSA's definition of "morally straight." He had grown up in the Scouts, joining when he was 11 and rising to Eagle Scout—the highest rank in the organization, reached by only 3 percent of the members. He also taught Sunday School at a local Lutheran church and after turning 18 remained involved with his troop as an assistant scoutmaster. "Boy Scouts was community," Dale told a reporter for *Rolling Stone*. "It was a place where I felt I belonged. I did other things. I was in soccer and basketball. But nothing fit as well as the Boy Scouts. I didn't have to be the best football player or run the fastest. In the Boy Scouts, I could be who I was. They valued me for who I was."

Or, at least Dale *thought* BSA valued him for who he was. At the age of 19, after leaving for college at Rutgers University, James Dale came out. He joined a campus lesbian and gay support organization, and was elected president of the group in his sophomore year. This made Dale the most visible of the organization's members; eventually, he attended an event that was covered by a local newspaper. A photograph identifying Dale as a gay rights leader ran in the paper, which alerted BSA officials that one of the organization's assistant scoutmasters was homosexual. He soon received a letter from BSA informing him that he had been expelled from the Scouts. "It was like a kidney punch," he told *Rolling Stone*. "I felt betrayed. This was the organization that taught me how to be me."

Dale sued the Scouts, claiming the organization discriminates against gays. After losing in a lower court, Dale appealed to the New Jersey Supreme Court, which found in his favor, ruling that BSA violated a state law banning discrimination based on sexual orientation. Still, James Dale was not permitted to return to the Boy Scouts. BSA appealed to the federal courts, which tied the case up for years. Finally, in 2000 — 10 years after Dale was kicked out of the Scouts — the nation's highest court ruled that the BSA, as a private organization, is permitted to bar membership to whomever it chooses. In the court's majority opinion, Chief Justice William H. Rehnquist wrote, "The forced inclusion of an unwanted person in a group infringes the group's freedom of expressive association if the presence of that person affects in a significant way the group's

Eagle Scout James Dale was expelled from the Scouts in 1990, when BSA officials learned that the assistant scoutmaster was also a member of a college gay and lesbian organization. In 2000, the U.S. Supreme Court ruled that the Boy Scouts were legally permitted to exclude homosexuals.

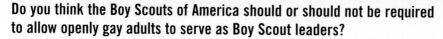

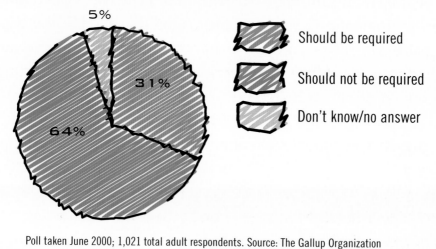

Do you think the Boy Scouts of America should or should not be required to allow openly gay adults to serve as Boy Scout leaders?

5%

31%

64%

- Should be required
- Should not be required
- Don't know/no answer

Poll taken June 2000; 1,021 total adult respondents. Source: The Gallup Organization

ability to advocate public or private viewpoints."

The BSA won the battle against gays, but it may take the organization years to recover from the war. In the years following the U.S. Supreme Court ruling, membership in the BSA dropped by nearly 5 percent. Many of the young people who left are heterosexuals who disagreed with the ban, believing that gays should have the right to join the BSA. Some 70 current and former Eagle Scouts quit, including the movie director Steven Spielberg, who had been a longtime BSA board member.

What's more, the Scouts lost some of their major funding sources. Many local United Way chapters, whose rules prohibit donating money to groups that discriminate, withdrew their financial support for the Boy Scouts. Municipalities and school districts that for years permitted the Scouts to use their facilities free of charge withdrew those offers, in many cases banning the Scouts entirely from their facilities.

The Boys Scouts of America remains one of the few youth-related groups in the United States that prohibits gay members. It is also one of the few youth-related groups in U.S. society with a declining membership. The Campfire Boys and Girls as well as the Boys and Girls Clubs of America do not prohibit gays. The national headquarters of the Girl Scouts leaves the question of whether to permit lesbian leaders and members in the hands of the local councils. About two dozen local Girl Scouts councils have responded by adopting resolutions specifically prohibiting discrimination based on sexual orientation; the others generally permit lesbians to participate in the Girl Scouts, although the organization maintains a national policy prohibiting leaders from advocating personal lifestyles. And the Canadian version of the Boy Scouts, known as Scouts Canada, does not discriminate based on sexual orientation. In fact, in 1999 a Scouts Canada troop known as the Toronto Rover Crew was formed specifically for gay and lesbian members.

Surveying the present state of the Boy Scouts of America, Boy Scout Kevin Elliot from Riverside, California, who appeared on the cover of *Newsweek* in 2001, told the magazine, "I think discrimination within the Boy Scouts gets rid of the whole concept of what the Boy Scouts are all about." And Phil Moshir, a Boy Scout leader from Big Flats, New York, told *Rolling Stone*, "There are a lot of good people out there who have a lot to offer to Scouting, no matter what their sexual preference. Just because someone is gay, it doesn't mean he'll force the gay lifestyle onto a boy. And having different kinds of people opens doors. It allows the boys to see how other people live. And they shouldn't be sheltered from this."

Chapter Six

Pop stars Britney Spears and Madonna kiss onstage during the 2003 MTV Music Video Awards. Female bisexuality has become a stylish way for rebellious teens to shock people.

Bisexual Chic

In 2003, a Russian singing duo known as t.A.T.u. scored a hit in the United States with the song "All the Things She Said." Members of t.A.T.u. are teenagers Lena Katina and Julia Volkova. They were recruited for the group by Russian record producer Ivan Shapovalov who explained to the on-line magazine Slate.msn.com the concept he had in mind for t.A.T.u.: "Every time, the audience needs new images—for this project, new images were lesbian teenagers."

In English, the Russian words whose initials spell t.A.T.u. translate into "This girl loves that girl." The video produced for "All the Things She Said" includes many images of Lena and Julia dressed in schoolgirl uniforms; they embrace, walk hand in hand, and kiss. The song as well as the video scored well with audiences. In Great Britain, the song hit the top of the charts; in the United States, "All the Things She Said" climbed into *Billboard* magazine's top 20. The video did even better, making it into the

Top 10 of MTV's *Total Request Live*. Why were the song and video so popular? In an interview with MTV News, Lena said, "We are singing about our love. Love between girl and girl."

Well, not quite. While there is no question that Lena and Julia certainly looked like lesbians, the truth is they were faking. Newspapers in Russia and elsewhere published many stories about Lena and Julia being seen around town in the company of their boyfriends. What Ivan Shapovalov discovered, though, is that it can be chic for teenage girls to be bisexual.

Anybody watching MTV's nationally televised Music Video Awards show in the summer of 2003 learned all about bisexual chic when, during the show, the pop singers Madonna, Britney Spears, and Christina Aguilera sang and danced together, then finished their performance by sharing long, affectionate kisses. Later, Britney told a reporter for CNN that the kiss was just "performing and expressing myself." She denied that she is a lesbian and said she would probably never kiss another woman.

When stars such as Madonna and Britney lock lips, young people undoubtedly pay attention. Both stars have been named in Gallup Youth Surveys as influential and popular role models for young people. It is possible that the impromptu kissing scene between Madonna and Britney Spears sent a message to teenage girls that same-sex shows of affection are acceptable behavior, but it is also possible that by the time Madonna and Britney kissed on national TV, many teenage girls were already doing it on their own.

Bisexuality Sells

Experts believe there are a number of reasons teenage girls experiment with bisexuality. True, some girls try it because of the example of pop stars like Britney, Christina, and the girls from t.A.T.u. Denise Pell, president of the bisexual advocacy group BiNet USA, told the *London Observer*, "Obviously if you are seeing pop icons or role models doing this, and they are OK with it, then you will feel more comfortable with it yourself."

Some girls experiment with bisexuality for shock value, taking part in the age-old teenage custom of doing something unusual simply to be rebellious. Other girls experiment with bisexuality to *titillate* their boyfriends. Many teenagers tell stories of going to parties where a group of boys encourage two girls to kiss in public. Many times, girls are only too happy to oblige. "Girls go for the whole mystery thing," Florida high school senior David Sternberg told the *Orlando Sun-Sentinel*. "And guys usually think it's attractive. It's a turn-on. It's more of a teasing thing. At parties, girls randomly kiss, and guys [say] like, 'Oh! That's awesome!'"

Advertising executives have even recognized the value of bisexual chic. Consider the case of Miller Brewing Company's

The duo t.A.T.u. were promoted as lesbians, but it was soon revealed that their pretended relationship was a calculated way to draw attention.

controversial updating of its "Tastes Great-Less Filling" commercials. Back in the 1970s, when the commercials first aired, the spots typically featured a couple of ex-jocks sitting across a bar, arguing the question of whether Miller Lite beer was better because of its taste or because of its propensity to make the drinker feel less bloated. By the time the campaign was revived more than two decades later, the ads had taken on a decidedly different twist. Fans tuning

TRANSGENDER YOUTHS: NO LONGER ON THE FRINGE

Brown University student Luke Woodward was born a woman, but feels more comfortable living life as a man. So she adopted a man's name and also had surgery to remove her breasts. "My quality of life is better," Luke told a reporter for the *New York Times*. Dressing like a man, acting like a man, Luke even uses the men's bathrooms on campus. Another transgender college student, Zachary Strassburger, is also a woman who adopted a man's name. She told the *New York Times*, "Some people think it's important to be seen as a specific gender; that's not me." Young transgenders include women like Luke and Zachary as well as men who dress in women's clothing— sometimes called "drag queens." (The term "drag" comes from the phrase "dressed as a girl.") Once believed to be on the fringe of gay society, transgenders have fought hard for acceptance and, to some degree, have won it.

Harvard University professor Marjorie Garber, author of *Vested Interests: Cross-Dressing and Cultural Anxiety*, told the *Boston Globe*: "We're seeing more cross-dressing right now because we're in a time of social upheaval. The current roles of men and women in society, maleness and femaleness and personality, are all very much under question." In other words, Garber says, the traditional roles of men and women have merged in recent years; for some people, that merger includes wearing each other's clothes or even having surgery to adopt a different gender. At least in gay circles, transgenders into the NFL playoffs in early 2003 would often see Miller Lite's so-called "Catfight" commercial, which featured two young men conjuring up an image of two beautiful women fighting over the merits of Miller Lite, eventually ripping off each other's clothes to settle the issue. At the conclusion of one version of the fight, with the Tastes Great-Less Filling controversy still not settled, one of the semi-naked girls asks the other, "Want to make out?" The commercial ends on a comic note, with the boys' dates looking on, horrified,

are accepted as part of the movement. Boys in drag compete for prom queen at gay proms. At Brown and Wesleyan universities as well as Smith and Sarah Lawrence colleges, transgender students have won some accommodations in their housing as well as permission to play on sports teams that do not require them to reveal their sexual identities.

It is important to point out that transgenders are not necessarily gay. Toronto psychologist Ken Zucker told the *New York Times*, "Gender identity is distinct from sexual orientation. Gender identity pertains to how a person feels about being male or female; sexual orientation pertains to who you are attracted to sexually."

There is no question, though, that young people who dress in drag face risks. If a gay boy is likely to experience abuse and physical threats in high school merely because he is gay, imagine the dangers he might face if he shows up for class in a skirt and high heels. In 2002, 17-year-old Eddie Araujo of Newark, California, went to a party dressed as a woman. Eddie, who preferred to be called "Gwen," was murdered after three young men found out he was male. According to Eddie's mother, Sylvia Guerrero, her son's death was simply another sad chapter in a life of harassment and abuse. "I could see the pain in his eyes," Guerrero told the *Advocate*. "People were really mean to him at school. He really tried, but no one accepted him."

although the guys seem oblivious to their girlfriends' icy stares.

"Every time I see it, I cringe," Atlanta advertising executive Laura Ries told *USA Today*. "It's explicit. It's degrading. It has no real message, except all men are idiots and all they think about are girls mud wrestling." Of course, the whole purpose of the ad is to titillate men and make them remember the Miller Lite brand when they are buying beer. Miller Brewing executives vigorously defended the Catfight ad. "[Men] see it for what it is: a hysterical insight into guys' mentality. It's really a lighthearted spoof of guys' fantasies," Miller brand manager Tom Bick told *USA Today*.

Still, experts are not sure that sort of behavior is healthy. They argue that girls who are unsure of their sexuality may find answers by experimenting with lesbian partners, but if they experiment at the invitation of their boyfriends, then they are simply letting themselves be controlled. Donna Yarbrough, director of the Lesbian Gay Bisexual Transgender Center at Tufts University in Massachusetts, told her school newspaper, "I think that generally these images reinforce the idea that women's sexual desire doesn't really exist except in relation to heterosexual men. 'Lesbian sexuality' is always presented and interpreted in the mainstream media as a performance for heterosexual men."

Girls Understand Girls

There are, of course, girls who experiment with lesbianism because they are truly unsure of their sexuality. Many of them have been through bad experiences with their boyfriends and are seeking somebody who is more nurturing, more sympathetic, more sensitive, and less self-centered. Boys who fit that mold are often hard to find; girls, however, often turn out to be just what girls are looking for. "Girls understand how girls think," Beltsville,

Maryland, high school student Chandra Harris told the *Washington Post*. "You can tell a girl, 'I think I'm falling in love with you' and she'll listen. A boy will slough that off, or run away." Adds Bladensburg, Maryland, student Kateria Rhodes: "It's not the sex. Girls are there for you emotionally. Sure, they cheat sometimes, but I've found [dating girls] is better for me mentally. Actually, it's better on every level."

Researchers point out that there is little substantial research on what causes girls to become lesbians. (The LaVay, Bailey-Pillard,. and Hamer studies all concentrated on gay men.) One of the few studies on lesbian trends was conducted by psychology professor Lisa Diamond at the University of Utah, who chronicled the sexual habits of a group of women between the ages of 16 and 23 over an eight-year period. Diamond found that two-thirds of the women she studied constantly changed their sexual orientations, going from straight to bisexual to lesbian a number of times. In an interview with the *Washington Post*, Diamond called them "heteroflexible." Diamond concluded that, unlike most gay men, some women are capable of changing their sexual orientation.

The true victims of bisexual chic may be women who are truly bisexual—women who are no longer questioning their sexuality but have, in fact, decided that they can share intimate moments with partners of both genders. They may look at t.A.T.u., Britney, Madonna, and Christina shocking their audiences and feel as though a lifestyle they regard as legitimate is being lampooned. Denise Pell of BiNet USA told the *Orlando Sun-Sentinel*: "It's important to take bisexuality as a serious identity. It's a myth that it is just a phase."

Chapter Seven

Advocates of gay rights participate in a 1993 demonstration in New York. The protesters were objecting to the Clinton administration's policy of permitting homosexuals to serve in the military as long as they did not disclose their sexual orientation.

Victories Measured in Inches and Miles

Ryan is a member of the U.S. Army. Like many U.S. soldiers since September 11, 2001, he was stationed in a war zone—in his case, while the United States was waging a war against Iraq. Ryan, who served six months in the Middle East, saw combat while his army unit was working to stabilize the volatile country after the war ended in April 2003. Ryan is unlike most other U.S. soldiers in one respect, however—he is gay.

Ryan refused to provide his last name to journalists because doing so would violate the U.S. military's "don't ask, don't tell" policy when it comes to gays. Officially, gays are prohibited from serving in the armed forces. In 1993, President Bill Clinton sought to end the policy banning gays, but he ran into fierce opposition from military leaders. So Clinton reached a compromise with the military: gays could serve as long as they kept their sexual orientations to themselves and did not display homosexual behavior on duty. In return, the military would not ask enlistees about their sexual orientations. Nobody would be asked, and nobody had a duty to tell. If gay soldiers violated the policy, though, they faced dismissal from the service. By 2004, some 10,000 members of the army, navy, air force, and marines had been discharged for violating the provisions of "don't ask, don't tell."

At the time the terms of "don't ask, don't tell" were being negotiated, some military leaders questioned whether homosexuals could be effective fighters. They wondered whether gay partners serving in the same unit would compromise the safety of everyone else. In an essay published in the *New York Times*, retired U.S. Army General Bernard E. Trainor and U.S. Marine Colonel Eric L. Chase wrote, "With openly gay and heterosexual personnel together, sexual tension would fester 24 hours a day. Romantic interests, even if unconsummated, would shatter the bonds that add up to unit cohesion."

Another reason military leaders fought against inclusion of gays was due to a fear of homophobia. They wondered how members of a gay soldier's unit would react when they found out his sexual preference. Would they react with hostility, beating up the hapless soldier? As things turned out, the answer to that question is generally "no." Although cases of homophobia do occur on military bases and aboard ships — as they do everywhere else in U.S. society — Ryan found that the soldiers in his unit accepted him as a fellow combatant. (Ryan did confide in some of his friends, and said that most members of his unit knew his sexual orientation, but he did not tell anyone in authority.) "It was a non-factor. Especially in a combat situation, it's really the last thing on anyone's mind. It's just a question of doing your job," Ryan said in a statement released by the Center for the Study of Sexual

Do you think people who are openly gay or homosexual should or should not be allowed to serve in the U.S. military?

3%

18%

79%

- Yes, should
- No, should not
- Don't know/no response

Poll taken December 2003; 1,004 total respondents. Source: The Gallup Organization

Minorities in the Military based at the University of California at Santa Barbara.

Ryan, who is president of the gay activist organization Gay and Lesbian Servicemembers for Equality, has lobbied Congress to repeal the "don't ask, don't tell" rule and permit gays to serve openly. Ryan and other activists point out that the U.S. military is for the most part alone in requiring gays to remain in the closet while they are in uniform. The British military, which fought alongside the Americans in Iraq, does permit gays to serve openly. In fact, gay activists point out, there were several occasions during the Iraq war in which British and American soldiers served side-by-side in combat. Quoted in the newspaper *East Bay Voice*, Massachusetts Congressman Martin Meehan said, "The adherents to the ban have never been able to produce any evidence that allowing gay men and lesbians to serve openly and honorably would harm the effectiveness of our military. The Iraq war demonstrates that the morale and cohesion of our forces is simply not affected by the presence of openly gay soldiers."

Ryan notes that while he was serving in the Middle East, his life and the lives of his fellow soldiers were often in danger. As a result, the soldiers in his unit learned to rely on one another. It was that level of trust, Ryan says, that helped keep soldiers alive during those dangerous months. "A great deal of military service is being able to trust the people around you," he said, "being able to be comfortable enough around them that you can trust someone with your life. . . . Having to conceal something like [one's sexual orientation] can make you doubt the personal bonds and professional bonds that you have with people. Lying makes it hard for others to trust you. . . . if you're living a lie, they're not trusting you, but a picture of you that you put in their head."

However, the "don't ask, don't tell" policy is not likely to be changed in the near future. There is little support in the higher echelons of the U.S. military or in Congress for altering the policy.

Some gays believe they deserved the right to serve as openly homosexual soldiers and remain bitter that the Clinton and Bush administrations did not go far enough to preserve their rights. But others regarded "don't ask, don't tell" as something of a victory for gays, given the fact that prior to the establishment of the rule they were completely banned from serving in the armed forces. Just as the Clinton administration was preparing to announce the "don't ask, don't tell" policy, a federal appeals court ordered the U.S. Navy to reinstate Joseph Steffan, a gay student who had been expelled from the Naval Academy. Steffan had committed no misconducts while at the Naval Academy and was, in fact, academically among the top 10 midshipmen in his class. He was kicked out simply for being gay. At the time the court order was announced, Steffan told reporters he was eager to rejoin the navy. Evan Wolfson, an attorney for the LAMBDA Legal Defense Fund, which represented Steffan, told the *Wall Street Journal*, "The court is saying that it is simply un-American to punish people for their desires, their thoughts and, therefore, their orientation, rather than their conduct."

Decriminalizing Homosexuality

As gay youth leave high school and college, they will find themselves confronted with a society wrestling with how best to observe their rights. There is no question, though, that across the spectrum of American life, gays are winning acceptance and rights they have never enjoyed before. Sometimes—as the case of military service shows—victories are measured in inches rather than miles. Another place where gays are winning just minor victories is the legalization of same-sex marriages. Some communities have declared their willingness to accept gays as legally married couples while many others have taken steps to prevent same-sex unions.

Sometimes, though, victories can be measured in miles. The 2003 U.S. Supreme Court decision dismissing *sodomy* between consenting partners as a crime is one such case. At the time, Texas and 12 other states maintained laws on their books making homosexual sex a crime—even if the act was consensual and performed in the privacy of a home. The challenge to the anti-sodomy law was initiated in 1998 by John Geddes Lawrence and Tyron Garner, two gay men who were having sex in their Harris County, Texas, home when police arrived to investigate the false report of an armed man inside the home. Instead, they arrested Lawrence and

Do you think marriages between homosexuals should or should not be recognized by the law as valid, with the same rights as traditional marriages?

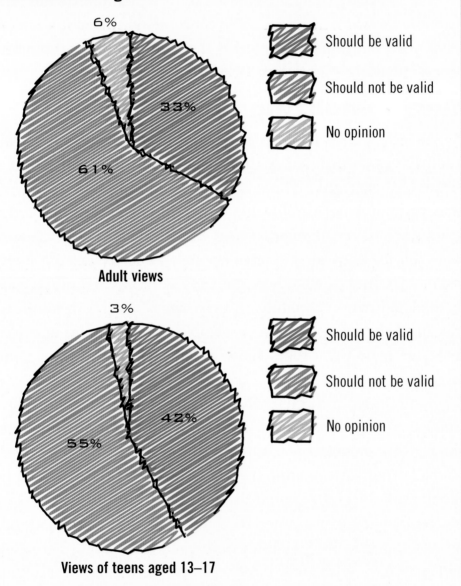

6%

33%

61%

Should be valid

Should not be valid

No opinion

Adult views

3%

42%

55%

Should be valid

Should not be valid

No opinion

Views of teens aged 13–17

Polls taken March 2004 (1,005 total adult respondents) and August 2003 (517 total teen respondents). Source: The Gallup Organization

Garner, charging them with violating Texas' anti-sodomy law. Lawrence and Garner were each fined $200, but the two men appealed and the case eventually reached the U.S. Supreme Court, which declared anti-sodomy laws to be an unconstitutional infringement on the right to privacy. Wrote Supreme Court Justice Anthony Kennedy, "The state cannot demean their existence or control their destiny by making their private sexual conduct a crime."

The Supreme Court order dissolved all remaining sodomy laws still on the books in the United States. Since there were just 13 states with such laws remaining, one can assume that policing people's sex habits was clearly not a priority for most state and local governments. Even the states that elected to keep the laws on the books hardly ever bothered to enforce them.

The 2003 decision overturned a 1986 Supreme Court order upholding the rights of states to pass anti-sodomy laws. That case was based on a challenge to an anti-sodomy law in Colorado, which the Supreme Court let stand. Ironically, prior to the 2003 Supreme Court decision, authorities in Colorado had jettisoned the anti-sodomy law on their own. Essentially, then, in 2003 the Supreme Court put its stamp of approval on a trend to **decriminalize** homosexuality that most Americans had already accepted on their own.

Million-Mile Journey

As an audience of about 100 friends and other well-wishers looked on, David Wilson and Robert Compton held hands inside the Arlington Street Church in Boston during May 2004. "I promise to love you, comfort and encourage you," Wilson told his long-time partner as the two men, dressed in dark suits and matching pink-and-red ties, exchanged wedding vows. "And now, by the power vested in me by the Commonwealth of Massachusetts, I hereby pronounce you partners for life," said the Reverend Kim Crawford Harvie, as the church exploded in applause.

The two men had lived together for nine years but had been barred by law from becoming legally married. That changed on May 17, 2004, when same-sex marriages became legal in Massachusetts. Wilson and Compton, who sued to win the right to marry, were among the first gay couples to legally exchange vows. After the ceremony, Wilson told the wedding guests, "In a journey that seemed like a million miles and had a million speed bumps, the Commonwealth of Massachusetts will finally recognize our family."

The issue of whether gay people should marry has deeply divided Americans. Many people think the institution of marriage should be a sacred bond shared only by a man and a woman. In fact, by 2004 38 states had passed so-called "Defense of Marriage" laws, specifically outlawing same-sex marriages and declaring that no same-sex union that is legal in another state would be recognized as legal within their borders. In 2004, President George W. Bush called for a constitutional amendment banning same-sex unions.

Marriage represents more than simply a state government's legal sanction to a couple's decision to live together. Married people enjoy certain benefits guaranteed by governments and society specifically designed to ensure that healthy families can prosper. For example, surviving spouses do not have to pay inheritance taxes on the money left to them when a husband or wife dies. Health insurance provided by employers is usually extended to a worker's spouse, as well as the children in the family. When a

In February 2004, San Francisco Mayor Gavin Newsom ordered that marriage licenses could be issued to same-sex couples. These women standing on the steps of the San Francisco courthouse were among the more than 4,100 couples who applied for the licenses, even though opponents said they were illegal because they violated state law.

retired worker dies, a spouse can continue to collect the worker's pension. When Massachusetts legalized same-sex unions, all those benefits were extended to gay couples.

Many conservative political and religious leaders are appalled at the idea of same-sex unions. As gay couples lined up in Massachusetts to apply for marriage licenses, lawmakers in Georgia, Kentucky, Mississippi, Oklahoma, Missouri, and Utah

REASONS SOME AMERICANS ARE OPPOSED TO SAME-SEX MARRIAGE

As gays and lesbians continue to fight for the legal right to marry, others have argued against the legalization of gay marriage. Many people are opposed on religious grounds, because the major faiths in the United States—Christianity, Judaism, and Islam—teach that homosexuality is a sin. To devout believers, therefore, allowing gay marriage would therefore condone sin. In addition, some people feel gay marriage would have a negative effect on society by weakening its basic structures—the institutions of marriage and the family. In an editorial that appeared in a February 2004 issue of *Christianity Today*, college religion teachers Robert Benne and Gerald McDermott gave three major reasons they believe this thesis.

First, the authors note that historically the term *marriage* has meant the lifelong monogamous union of a man and a woman. "Any other arrangement contradicts the basic definition," Benne and McDermott explained. "Scrambling the definition of marriage will be a shock to our fundamental understanding of human social relations and institutions. One effect will be that sexual fidelity will be detached from the commitment of marriage." They point to a study from the Netherlands, where gay marriage is legal, that found that even among stable slated *referenda* asking voters to approve amendments to state constitutions banning same-sex marriages. James Dobson, founder of the conservative Christian lobbying group Focus on the Family, told an Associated Press reporter, "The documents being issued all across Massachusetts may say 'marriage license' at the top but they are really death certificates for the institution of marriage."

According to the Gallup Youth Survey, a majority of young people oppose same-sex unions. In 2003, 517 teens between the ages of 13 and 17 were asked, "Do you approve or disapprove of

homosexual partnerships, men had an average of eight partners per year outside their relationship. "In short," they wrote, "gay marriage will change marriage more than it will change gays."

Second, if gay marriage is legalized Benne and McDermott believe that a primary purpose of marriage as defined in the Bible—raising children—will become less important than the adult relationship. "Acceptance of gay marriage will strengthen the notion that marriage is primarily about adult yearnings for intimacy and is not essentially connected to raising children," they wrote. They also pointed to an article in the journal *Child Trends* about how the makeup of a family affects the children in that family. According to this article, the optimal family structure is one in which the biological mother and father raise the children in a low-conflict environment.

Finally, they argue, the effects described above "will have strong repercussions on a society that is already having trouble maintaining wholesome stability in marriage and family life. If marriage and families are the foundation for a healthy society, introducing more uncertainty and instability in them will be bad for society."

marriages between homosexuals?" A total of 42 percent approved while 55 percent said they did not approve. The same poll asked young people whether they favor mixed-race marriage; 86 percent of the respondents approved. Further, 93 percent said they approve of marriages between Jews and non-Jews, while 92 percent said they approve of marriages between Hispanics and non-Hispanics. This data suggests that young people are willing to accept mixed marriages involving different races, religions, and ethnicities, but they are hesitant to grant similar approval to gays.

In addition, the Gallup Youth Survey found girls more open-minded than boys on the issue of gay unions. Fifty-six percent of the girls who responded to the poll said they support same-sex marriages, while only 30 percent of the boys said they approve of gay unions. Younger teens also seemed to be more willing to accept gay unions. Forty-five percent of the respondents between the ages of 13 and 15 said they could approve of gay weddings, while just 38 percent of the 16- and 17-year-old teens said they approve of same-sex unions.

Teenagers who regularly attend church are far less willing to accept gays as legally wedded spouses. The Gallup Youth Survey found just 29 percent of churchgoing teens in favor of same-sex marriage while 53 percent of teens who do not regularly attend church said they could approve of gay marriage. A similar Gallup Youth Survey conducted in 2000 showed Roman Catholic teens are more likely to approve gay marriage than Protestants, with 60 percent of Catholic young people and 36 percent of Protestant teens endorsing same-sex unions.

If gays can marry, can they also raise children? Donald and Earl Snyder of Lower Nazareth, Pennsylvania, exchanged vows in 2001, although Pennsylvania does not legally recognize gay unions. Nevertheless, they consider themselves spouses; following their "wedding" Earl changed his last name to Snyder. "It's a marriage under God, but it's not legal in Pennsylvania," Donald Snyder told the *Allentown Morning Call*. The Snyders have also adopted a baby boy, which is legal in Pennsylvania and elsewhere. Teenagers believe, by a narrow margin, that gay couples like the Snyders should have the right to adopt. The 2003 Gallup Youth Survey found that 51 percent of the respondents favor the right of gay people to adopt children while 46 percent do not believe they should adopt children. Church-going teens are far less willing to support gay adoption, with just 36 percent favoring the right of gay partners to become adoptive parents, while 62 percent of teens who do not regularly attend church believe gay people have the right to be adoptive parents. More girls than boys favor gay adoption, with 62 percent of girls and 40 percent of boys endorsing the right of gay people to adopt children.

The state legislature in Massachusetts legalized same-sex unions in response to a state Supreme Court order in a case brought in 2000 by Compton and Wilson as well as six other gay couples who had been denied marriage licenses in Massachusetts. The Massachusetts Supreme Court ruled in November 2003 that the state's refusal to grant marriage licenses to the couples violated gay people's rights and they subsequently gave the government six months to make the licenses available to same-sex couples.

As the state government in Massachusetts prepared to make licenses available to gay couples, other communities—emboldened by the Massachusetts ruling—decided to test their own state laws. City and county officials in Sandoval, New Mexico, New Palitz, New York, and Asbury Park, New Jersey, attempted to issue marriage licenses to gay couples, but state legal authorities

stepped in and halted them with threats of arrest and other sanctions. In San Francisco—a city with the largest population of gays in America—Mayor Gavin Newsom directed city authorities to issue marriage licenses to gay couples, and more than 4,100 licenses were issued before state officials won a court order temporarily halting the practice. California's voters had approved a "Defense of Marriage" law in 2000 and opponents to gay marriage argued that San Francisco's decision to issue marriage licenses to homosexuals violated the statute. On August 12, 2004, the California Supreme Court ruled that the same-sex marriages performed in San Francisco had violated state law and were therefore not valid, and that the mayor could not issue marriage licenses to gay and lesbian couples.

There is no question that gay people are winning broader rights, albeit sometimes quite slowly. It means that for the gay teenager who endures verbal or physical harassment in high school, there is hope for equality. For the young person wondering how to tell her parents that she is gay, there are role models to follow. For the teenager wondering why he is gay, there is now scientific evidence that is beginning to provide answers. For the young gay person who is depressed or suicidal, there are books written for them by sympathetic authors who understand what they are going through and have created protagonists to help show them the way. And for young gay people who emerge into society, there is the chance they will one day receive the same benefits that are guaranteed to heterosexuals. During the few weeks that San Francisco officials issued marriage licenses to gays, among the first people to apply were lesbians Phyllis Lyon, 79, and Del Martin, 83. Lyon and Martin had waited 51 years for permission to marry. Surveying the long line of couples waiting behind them to apply for marriage licenses, Lyon told a reporter for the *Washington Post*: "This marriage thing is going to spread and spread and spread."

Glossary

ADULTERY—sexual intercourse between a married person and a non-spouse.

ANTI-HATE CRIME LAWS—laws set up to prosecute individuals who engage in various crimes (such as assault or defacement of property) when motivated by hostility to the victim as a member of a group based on color, creed, gender, or sexual orientation.

ATHEISTS—persons who do not believe in the existence of God.

BIGAMY—practice of a man or woman marrying more than one spouse; illegal in all states.

BISEXUAL—willing to have sexual relations with members of both genders.

CADAVERS—human corpses used for medical dissection.

CHROMOSOME—threadlike particle of a cell that carries genes.

DNA—deoxyribonucleic acid; chemical found in a cell that transmits hereditary traits.

DECRIMINALIZE—to remove or reduce the criminal classification or status of.

ESTROGEN—hormone produced in women's bodies that is responsible for breast and genital development and hair and fat distribution.

GENE—unit found on a chromosome that carries hereditary characteristics and through interaction with other genes controls hereditary development.

HETEROSEXUAL—willing to have sexual relations only with a member of the opposite gender.

HOMOPHOBIC—hatred or fear of gay people.

HYSTERECTOMY—surgical removal of the uterus, resulting in sterility of the woman; usually performed as a treatment for cancer or other illness.

Glossary

INCEST—sexual relations between close members of a family.

LESBIAN—female homosexual; the term stems from the name of the inhabitants of the ancient island of Lesbos whose poetry glorified love between women.

PHYSIOLOGICAL—characteristic of or appropriate to an organism's healthy or normal functioning.

POLYGAMY—similar to bigamy, but the husband or wife marries multiple partners at the same time.

PREJUDICES—preconceived preferences; bias.

PROMISCUOUS—engaging in sexual relations with many partners in a short period of time.

PSYCHIATRIC—pertaining to the medical study, diagnosis, treatment, and prevention of mental illness.

QUEER—once regarded as a derogatory term for homosexuality, gays now embrace the word as a proud and defiant description of their lifestyles.

REFERENDUM (PLURAL REFERENDA)—the practice of submitting to popular vote a question posed by a government body.

SODOMY—anal sex.

STEM CELL—an unspecified cell that gives rise to differentiated cells.

TITILLATE—to excite someone's sensations.

TRANSGENDER—to cross gender lines, usually by dressing as a member of the opposite gender.

Internet Resources

http://www.gallup.com

Visitors to the Internet site maintained by The Gallup Organization can find results of Gallup Youth Surveys as well as many other research projects undertaken by the national polling firm.

http://www.outproud.org

The results of OutProud's 1997 and 2000 surveys of gay teens can be accessed at the Internet site of the organization, which is based in San Raphael, California. Young people can also find coming out stories written by teens and links to libraries and on-line resources of gay interest.

http://www.glsen.org

The Gay, Lesbian and Straight Education Network (GLSEN) helps students form Gay-Straight Alliances in their schools. Visitors to the Web site can read news accounts of GLSEN's activities, access an archive of more than 1,000 articles on gay-related issues, and find contacts for GLSEN staff members who will work with students.

http://www.cdc.gov

Dozens of studies and articles about gay health issues as well as teen sexuality and its consequences are available on-line from the Centers for Disease Control and Prevention.

http://www.gaymilitary.ucsb.edu

Based at the University of California at Santa Barbara, the Center for the Study of Sexual Minorities in the Military researches the plight of gays in the American military. Visitors to the Web site can access a number of news articles and studies on the center's activities, and students with ideas for research projects can obtain information about obtaining grants from the center.

Internet Resources

http://www.homophobiainsports.com

News articles about gay athletes, the status of the project's legal cases, and reports from the organization's annual conference are available on the Homophobia in Sports Project'sWeb site. In addition, visitors can download the group's "It Takes A Team" poster.

http://www.advocate.com

The news magazine *The Advocate* maintains an extensive on-line archive of thousands of articles covering the full spectrum of gay issues. Visitors can also find links to gay rights groups, vote in *Advocate* polls, and participate in chat rooms.

http://www.hmi.org

The Hetrick-Martin Institute of New York maintains a Web site for the Harvey Milk High School. Visitors can see a gallery of photos of Harvey Milk students participating in school activities, read letters from gay students, post their own letters, and find statistics and other information on gay youth.

http://www.lambdalegal.org

Lawyers for the LAMBDA Legal Defense Fund represent gays who believe they are victims of discrimination.

http://www.ntac.org

The rights of transgenders are spelled out on the National Transgender Advocacy Coalition's World Wide Web page. Also, visitors can find news reports on transgenders who win battles against discrimination.

Further Reading

Berman, Louis A. *The Puzzle: Exploring the Evolutionary Puzzle of Male Homosexuality*. Wilmette, Ill.: Godot Press, 2003.

Bernstein, Robert A., Betty DeGeneres, and Robert MacNeill. *Straight Parents, Gay Children: Keeping Families Together*. New York: Thunder's Mouth Press, 2003.

Boyer, David. *Kings and Queens: Queers at the Prom*. New York: Soft Skull Press, 2004.

Dunbar, Robert E. *Issues in Focus: Homosexuality*. Springfield, N.J.: Enslow Publishers, 1995.

Garber, Marjorie. *Vested Interests: Cross-Dressing and Cultural Anxiety*. London: Rutledge, 1991.

Huegel, Kelly. *GLBTQ: The Survival Guide for Queer and Questioning Teens*. Minneapolis: Free Spirit Publishing, 2003.

Marcovitz, Hal. *Teens and Sex*. Philadelphia: Mason Crest Publishers, 2004.

———. *Teens and Suicide*. Philadelphia: Mason Crest Publishers, 2004.

McDougall, Bryce. *My Child is Gay: How Parents React When They Hear the News*. Chicago: Independent Publishers Group, 1998.

Savin-Williams, Ritch C. *Mom, Dad, I'm Gay: How Families Negotiate Coming Out*. Washington, D.C.: American Psychological Association, 2001.

Index

Numbers in **bold italic** refer to captions and graphs.

Index

Index

Picture Credits

Contributors

GEORGE GALLUP JR. is chairman of The George H. Gallup International Institute (sponsored by The Gallup International Research and Education Center, or GIREC) and is a senior scientist and member of the GIREC council. Mr. Gallup serves on many boards in the area of health, education, and religion.

Mr. Gallup is recognized internationally for his research and study on youth, health, religion, and urban problems. He has written numerous books including *My Kids On Drugs?* with Art Linkletter (Standard, 1981), *The Great American Success Story* with Alec Gallup and William Proctor (Dow Jones-Irwin, 1986), *Growing Up Scared in America* with Wendy Plump (Morehouse, 1995), *Surveying the Religious Landscape: Trends in U.S. Beliefs* with D. Michael Lindsay (Morehouse, 1999), and *The Next American Spirituality* with Timothy Jones (Chariot Victor Publishing, 1999).

Mr. Gallup received his BA degree from the Princeton University Department of Religion in 1954, and holds seven honorary degrees. He has received many awards, including the Charles E. Wilson Award in 1994, the Judge Issacs Lifetime Achievement Award in 1996, and the Bethune-DuBois Institute Award in 2000. Mr. Gallup lives near Princeton, New Jersey, with his wife, Kingsley. They have three grown children.

THE GALLUP YOUTH SURVEY was founded in 1977 by Dr. George Gallup to provide ongoing information on the opinions, beliefs and activities of America's high school students and to help society meet its responsibility to youth. The topics examined by the Gallup Youth Survey have covered a wide range—from abortion to zoology. From its founding through the year 2001, the Gallup Youth Survey sent more than 1,200 weekly reports to the Associated Press, to be distributed to newspapers around the nation. Since January 2002, Gallup Youth Survey reports have been made available on a weekly basis through the Gallup Tuesday Briefing.

HAL MARCOVITZ is a Pennsylvania-based journalist. He has written more than 50 books for young readers. His other titles for the Gallup Youth Survey series include *Teens and Career Choices* and *Teens and Volunteerism*. He lives in Chalfont, Pennsylvania, with his wife, Gail, and daughters Ashley and Michelle.